JUSTICE
AND
THE
SUPREME
COURT

Rocco J. Tresolini
*Professor of Political Science and
Head, Department of Government,
Lehigh University*

J. B. LIPPINCOTT COMPANY
PHILADELPHIA • NEW YORK

103771

For the blue-eyed girl who makes it all possible.

PREFACE

THIS BOOK, which is the outcome of several years' research on the lives and times of Supreme Court justices, has focused on the political and historical as well as the legal aspects of the Court's work. However, it is by no means to be construed as a final delineation of my researches to date. It represents a beginning rather than the completion of the project. Yet presentation of the book at this time seems appropriate, since nothing quite like it has been done before. Any comments, criticism, and suggestions from scholars and students as well as interested lay readers will be welcomed.

A number of persons and groups have helped in various ways to make this book possible. Several early drafts of the manuscript were patiently read and criticized by two of my colleagues at Lehigh: Professor Ernst B. Schulz and Dean W. Ross Yates. Their suggestions have improved the book considerably. Dr. Glenn J.

Christensen, Dean of the College of Arts and Science and Provost
and Vice-President at Lehigh, read various early drafts of the
manuscript and offered encouragement at critical stages in the
work. Over the years, Dr. Lawrence H. Gipson, Pulitzer prize-
winning historian at Lehigh, has provided constant encouragement through his comments, suggestions, and deep interest.

I profited immensely from comments and suggestions made by
a number of readers on specific chapters published as separate
papers. I am particularly indebted to the following: Professor
Henry J. Abraham, University of Pennsylvania; Professor Robert
G. Dixon, Jr., The George Washington University School of Law;
Professor Charles Fairman, Harvard Law School; Dr. Rodney L.
Mott, Colgate University; Mr. Sol Rabkin, Anti-Defamation
League of B'nai B'rith, New York; Dr. George D. Harmon, Le-
high University; Dr. Richard W. Taylor, Coe College; Dr. John
Vanderzell, Franklin and Marshall College.

James Malone, an undergraduate assistant, helped in the initial
collection of data. Later, Darold Hemphill and Howard Whit-
comb, both graduate assistants, also helped collect needed materials. Several drafts of the manuscript were carefully and patiently
typed by Miss Sandra K. Snellman and Mrs. Virginia Frey. Li-
brarians at the Biddle Law Library, University of Pennsylvania;
Lehigh University Library; Manuscript Division, Library of
Congress; and the National Archives were most cooperative in
answering questions and providing materials.

A faculty research fellowship granted by Lehigh during the
summer of 1960 enabled me to devote full time to the project
over a three-month period. During the past several years the Lehigh University Institute of Research has made grants in support
of several aspects of this work. During the summer of 1962 a
grant from the American Philosophical Society enabled me to
concentrate further on Justice Rutledge and the Yamashita case
discussed in Chapter 8.

As noted above, several chapters were first published as separate articles by various journals. Approximately one-half of Chap-

Preface

ter 2 first appeared in the *Northwest Ohio Quarterly*, vol. XXXIV, Summer, 1962. A substantial part of Chapter 3 was first published by *The Quarterly Review of Higher Education Among Negroes*, vol. XXX, January, 1962. Chapter 8 appeared in *Social Science*, vol. XXXVII, June, 1962. Much of Chapter 1 was first presented in the 1962 Senior Lecture Series at Lehigh and subsequently published with other papers delivered during the year. I have drawn heavily from my *American Constitutional Law*, Macmillan Company, 1959, for the materials in Appendix 4. I am grateful for permission to reproduce each of these here.

The names of a number of other persons who contributed data for individual chapters are noted in the appropriate chapter bibliographies. Finally, I am indebted to members of the College Staff of J. B. Lippincott Company for their early enthusiasm and faith in the manuscript.

Rocco J. Tresolini

Pleasant Valley, Pennsylvania
January, 1963

CONTENTS

CONTENTS

INTRODUCTION

IN RECENT YEARS the Supreme Court of the United States has become increasingly concerned with the protection of individual liberties. In fact, in our times, the Court can truly be characterized as the voice of the enlightened conscience of the American people. Amid much of the shabbiness and cynicism of American political life it has had the courage to give practical meaning to our highest ideals. In the past few years it has done more than any other organ of government to remind us of our fundamental freedoms. Yet, since 1937, the Court has been subjected to a series of attacks precisely because this interest in individual liberties has replaced laissez faire as a major concern of the nine justices. Nevertheless, it is already clear that the major work of the Court in our times will continue to revolve around the protection of human noneconomic liberties.

Writing two decades ago, Robert K. Carr, now President of

Oberlin College, remarked, "It is entirely possible that a careful examination of the personalities and the economic and social backgrounds of the eighty men who have served on the Supreme Court would prove to be as valuable and realistic an approach to the American Constitution as the more usual law school approach which lays so much emphasis upon the study of cases, the rule of stare decisis, and of fixed legal principles." [1] Since that time, judicial biography has been invigorated by a number of careful studies, but few of these materials have been incorporated into the textbooks in any systematic way. Neither is there time in most courses to expose the student to full-length biographical studies.

This book is designed to focus on the civil liberties aspects of the Court's work that are not found in textbooks ordinarily used in political science, citizenship, and history courses. It is intended as a supplement to courses in American government, constitutional law, civil liberties, citizenship, and American constitutional history. Moreover, every effort has been made to present the materials in a clear, interesting, and readable manner so that able secondary school students can use the book. During the past several years the National Council for the Social Studies and the Civil Liberties Educational Foundation as well as other groups have launched vigorous drives to strengthen the teaching of civil liberties in the secondary schools.

One of the major current obstacles to effective teaching of individual freedoms at this level is the insufficiency of good teaching materials. It is hoped that the approach of this book—concentration on the lives and activities of several justices of varied backgrounds and on the detailed study of a major opinion of each of them—will help meet that need by teaching students both something about the justices themselves and about the difficult problems that must be resolved in the decision-making process. This approach should stimulate students to read more com-

[1] Robert K. Carr, *The Supreme Court and Judicial Review* (New York: Rinehart, 1942), p. 235.

prehensive materials on Supreme Court justices and their important civil liberties decisions. It is also hoped that this work will prove of value to interested lay citizens and that it will call attention to the need for more concern with the fundamental principles that should guide Americans in the uncertain days ahead.

In the interest of readability, footnotes have been kept to an absolute minimum throughout the book. Some sources, particularly for long quotations and other materials, are indicated at the bottom of the appropriate page. The citations for the cases and sources for other data are found in the bibliographical notes provided at the back of the book. *All* the sources used are listed in the biographical notes so that those who wish to investigate further a particular justice or case may do so easily. A serious attempt has been made to go beyond the strictly written legal record. Wherever possible, the private papers of individual justices, newspaper and magazine accounts, correspondence with principals in the case, and interviews have been utilized to help enrich a number of the chapters.

As to the selection of justices and cases I console myself with the thought that no collection can ever satisfy everyone. Many factors, such as availability of extra-legal materials on both justices and specific cases, intrinsic teaching value of materials available, and a desire to present justices of varied interests and backgrounds, have helped dictate the choices made. Moreover, I have been partial to those justices who seemed more prepared, as one writer has said, "to face the tides of their own day, men to remind Americans of their basic values and damn the passions of the moment." [1] Eight justices—Chief Justices Roger B. Taney, Morrison R. Waite, and Charles Evans Hughes, and Justices John M. Harlan (first), Oliver W. Holmes, Hugo Black, Wiley Rutledge, and Frank Murphy—and eight of their more important majority or dissenting opinions in civil liberties cases are presented. In addition, the career of Chief Justice Earl Warren and

[1] John P. Frank, *Marble Palace* (New York: A. A. Knopf, 1958), p. 292.

his role in the crucial segregation cases of 1954 are discussed in Chapter 3.

Not all these men are considered "great" judges. Of this group, only Justice Holmes and Chief Justice Hughes have been consistently classified with the "great" ones such as John Marshall and Louis Brandeis. It is too early to even attempt a final evaluation of more recent members such as Justice Black and Chief Justice Warren. But the classification of justices into categories such as "great," "average," "mediocre," or "poor," by various scholars is, at present, extremely dangerous and quite meaningless. There is disagreement as to what constitutes greatness on the bench. In truth, no definitive conception of the "great" justice exists. In general, justices have been considered great if they contributed significantly to the life of the law and possessed traits such as political wisdom, high intellectual ability, disinterestedness, intellectual integrity, courage, imagination, and a flair for literary composition. Needless to say, it is difficult to find all or even a substantial number of such traits in any one man, whether he is on or off the bench. Most important, the passage of time may alter drastically the evaluations of a justice's influence and contributions.

Chief Justice Waite, for example, has seldom been classified as a "great" judge. His failure to gain a reputation is due, in part, to the fact that he was a modest, humble, nonpolitical man who was content to do his work competently without fanfare. Such qualities may be as valuable for the Supreme Court, if not more valuable on occasion than some of those usually required for "greatness." At various times Justice Murphy has been described by scholars as a "New Deal political hack," a "legal illiterate," and a "judicial misfit." Justice Murphy certainly was not "great" in the classic sense. Yet such vitriolic remarks obscure the fact that along with Justice Rutledge he was one of the most eloquent defenders of the American tradition of human freedom. His bold and compassionate opinions in the cause of freedom for all men may yet prove to be of more abiding influence on future controversies than those of his supposedly much more capable brethren.

If nothing else, this book should reveal that the judicial protection of individual freedom is not a new invention of the Court of the nineteen-fifties and sixties and that in the modern world we need the Court more than ever before. Precious liberties can easily be lost in an age of expediency and flexible administration; of confusion and fear of military disaster. The conclusions of a practicing attorney concerning the role of the Supreme Court in six cases involving the death penalty may well be applied in some degree to all civil liberties cases. He stated as follows:

The fact is that an active ingredient in the workings of one branch of the most powerful government on earth is compassion. Compassion for the fate of solitary people, of desperate, lonely, untutored, and disturbed people. Compassion for human life regardless of its extrinsic worth.

Is this feeling, shared in varying degrees by all members of the Supreme Court, merely "some fastidious squeamishness or private sentimentalism?"

I think not. I think that in the long pull of humanity, one of the phenomena most proudly recorded will be this extraordinary attempt, hardly articulated and yet forcefully manifest, to enhance human dignity through the protection of human life.[1]

[1] Barrett Prettyman, Jr., *Death and the Supreme Court* (New York: Harcourt, Brace and World, 1961), p. 311.

I

Chief Justice Roger B. Taney
and the Merryman Case

Of how a much abused, sick and dying Chief Justice challenged even Lincoln to protect the constitutional rights of a Confederate sympathizer.

THE MAN

NO JUSTICE OF THE Supreme Court has been more roundly denounced and so grossly misrepresented as was Roger Brooke Taney. He was bitterly condemned on various occasions during his many years in public life. Even his death failed to halt the torrent of unbridled criticism. Upon hearing of Taney's death in 1864, Charles Francis Adams wrote jubilantly to Henry Adams: "So old Taney is at last dead . . . the darling wish of Taney's last day is doomed not to be realized. It was not reserved for him to put the veto of law on the Proclamation of Emancipation." [1] Congress refused to pass a bill providing funds for a Taney bust in the courtroom. In opposing the bill, Charles Sumner rose on the Senate floor to proclaim, "The name of Taney is to be hooted down the page of history. Judgment is beginning now;

[1] Quoted in Walter P. Armstrong, "The Rehabilitation of Roger B. Taney," *Tennessee Law Review*, XIV (June, 1936), 206.

and an emancipated country will fasten upon him the stigma which he deserves. . . . He administered justice at least wickedly, and degraded the judiciary of the country, and degraded the age." [1]

Shortly after his death an article in the *Atlantic Monthly* said that Taney was disposed "to serve the cause of evil." A historian referred to Taney as "a vampire hovering in the dim twilight." Another writer of the period predicted that the "memory of the Chief Justice will gather blackness from exposure on the walls of Time: and that the outcry of man against him is destined to increase rather than abate." [2]

But though this unflattering picture of Taney persisted for many years, it is now clear that the judgment of his detractors will not prevail. Recent scholarship has demonstrated that Taney was a much better chief justice than his critics would have us believe. The new note was sounded in an address delivered by Chief Justice Hughes at the unveiling of a bust of Taney at Frederick, Maryland in 1931. On that occasion Hughes remarked aptly, "With the passing of the years, and the softening of old asperities, the arduous service nobly rendered by Roger Brooke Taney has received its fitting recognition. He bore his wounds with the fortitude of an invincible spirit. He was a great Chief Justice." [3]

Some fifteen years later Chief Justice Warren arrived at a similar estimate. Noting that the passions of the age had eclipsed Taney's greatness, Warren remarked that the true Taney has now emerged. "We know him to-day as a needed balance to Marshall's conservative nationalism; as one who personally detested slavery, but who detested even more the prospect of violent disunion. We know him to-day as a great Chief Justice." [4]

[1] *Congressional Globe*, 38th Congress, 2d Session, p. 1012.

[2] *The Unjust Judge: A Memorial of Roger Brooke Taney* (New York: Baker and Godwin, 1865), p. 68.

[3] Charles Evans Hughes, "Roger Brooke Taney," *American Bar Association Journal*, XVII (December, 1931), 790.

[4] Earl Warren, "Roger Brooke Taney: Fifth Chief Justice of the United States," *American Bar Association Journal*, XLI (June, 1955), 505.

Taney was born on a prosperous tobacco plantation in Calvert County, Maryland on March 17, 1777—within the year following the signing of the Declaration of Independence. Both his parents were stanch Roman Catholics and descendants of some of Maryland's earliest settlers. Through the years the families of each had continued to acquire both land and slaves so that by 1777 the Taney family was firmly entrenched in the landed aristocracy class of Maryland. The Maryland aristocrats were a proud and rather snobbish lot. They looked upon the Negro as property indispensable to the maintenance of the great estates. "They built fine plantation homes. They fashioned, borrowed, or stole coats of arms. They bred blooded fox hounds with which they scoured the country in the company of those of their neighbors who had likewise achieved the status of 'gentlemen.' Traveling up and down the streams of southern Maryland, they visited and entertained in great style, stimulating their awareness of the fact that they were the cream of society." [1]

It was in this social environment that Taney grew up. From his father he learned to swim, fish, ride, and hunt. But fox hunting and duck shooting never appealed to him very much. Throughout his life Taney was too frail and sickly to have much interest in such activities. He always seemed to be suffering from some ailment that made an active outdoor life impossible. But his love of the countryside, of flowers and quiet streams never abated. Someone has aptly said, "His love of the country was more that of the poet than that of the squire."

Taney's mother undoubtedly exerted the greatest influence on him. She was a warm, loving soul who helped him develop into a kind, thoughtful, and understanding person. In his partially completed memoirs Taney wrote that his mother was "pious, gentle and affectionate, retiring and domestic in her tastes. I never in my life heard her say an angry or unkind word to any of her children or servants, nor speak ill of anyone. When any of us or the servants about the house who were under her immedi-

[1] Carl B. Swisher, *Roger B. Taney* (New York: Macmillan, 1935), p. 3. Reprinted by permission.

ate control (all of whom were slaves) committed a fault, her re-
proof was gentle and affectionate. . . . I remember and feel the
effect of her teaching to this hour." [1] (September, 1854). It was
undoubtedly from his mother that Taney learned to treat slaves
with kindness and to begin to look upon slavery itself as perhaps
morally wrong.

Taney began school at eight years of age, walking three miles
with an older brother and sister to the log cabin home of a "well
disposed but ignorant old man, who professed to teach reading,
writing and arithmetic as far as the rule of three." [2] Later Taney
and his brother were sent to study Latin at a boarding school ten
miles from the Taney plantation. But after only two or three
months, the teacher became mentally ill and the school was
closed. Taney's father then hired a series of private tutors who
resided at the plantation and instructed all the children.

On the day the boy was born, Taney's father had decided that
his younger son should be a lawyer. Taney himself wrote in his
memoirs that law "was the profession my father had always desired me to follow, and which I myself preferred." Accordingly,
he was sent to Dickinson College in Carlisle, Pennsylvania and
upon graduation, began to read law in the office of a well-known
judge in Annapolis. An ambitious young man, Taney studied in-
tensely for three years and was admitted to the bar in 1799. That
same year, largely through the efforts of his father and his
planter friends, Taney was elected to the lower house of the
state legislature on the Federalist Party ticket. But the next year
he was defeated by the Jeffersonians along with John Adams and
other leading Federalists in the state. Taney was stunned by the
Republican victory. He wrote that both he and his father were
"mortified at the defeat. It put an end to any prospect of immediate political elevation."

---

[1] Taney's account of his life and personal letters appears in Samuel Tyler,
Memoir of Roger Brooke Taney (Baltimore: John Murphy, 1872), pp. 17-
95. The description of his mother appears on pp. 26-27.
[2] *Ibid.*, p. 27.

After several long discussions with his father, Taney decided in 1801 to move to Frederick where the two best-known lawyers in the community were about to retire from practice. He lived and practiced law in Frederick for over twenty years. It was there that he met and married Anne Phoebe Key, the sister of Francis Scott Key, whom Taney had first known in Annapolis. Though Anne Key was a devout Episcopalian rather than a Roman Catholic like her husband, religious disagreement never marred the marriage. In fact, "It was a happy marriage and most fortunate for Taney. It seems probable, in view of his fragile health and easily shattered nervous system, that his long life and professional achievements would have been impossible without the solicitous care and devotion of his wife and the daughters who were born to them." [1]

In Frederick, Taney's reputation as an honest and able lawyer grew through the years. He also dabbled in politics, serving as state senator from 1816 to 1821. But soon Frederick became too small and provincial for an ambitious man who still wanted to make a bigger mark in the world. In 1823 Taney moved to Baltimore where he quickly emerged as one of the best-known lawyers in the state. Four years later he was appointed Attorney General of Maryland.

Taney had originally been a stanch Federalist, but he soon became an active supporter of Andrew Jackson. The seemingly giant step to Jacksonianism was not too difficult for Taney. His own party was dead. In Jackson and the Democrats Taney saw the "best prospect of maintaining the rural culture which he loved." Moreover, Jackson "was a landed aristocrat and owner of slaves in the tradition of the Taneys." In 1831 his political service to Jackson was rewarded with an appointment as Attorney General of the United States. From that time until his death, Taney remained a leading figure in national politics.

Taney played an important role in the Jackson cabinet. Moreover, he became one of Jackson's warmest friends and his most

[1] Swisher, *op. cit.*, p. 50.

trusted advisor. In 1833 Jackson named Taney Secretary of the
Treasury after two previous secretaries had refused to aid Jackson in his spectacular battle with the Bank of the United States.
As Secretary, Taney, who had long been opposed to the moneyed
aristocracy, was only too happy to cripple the bank and almost
immediately ordered the withdrawal of deposits of the federal
government. His action was severely criticized by the National
Republicans in Congress. Under the leadership of Senators Webster and Clay, the Senate struck back by refusing to confirm
Taney's appointment as Secretary of the Treasury. Less than a
year later the Senate refused to confirm his appointment as Associate Justice of the Supreme Court.

In the meantime, Taney had returned to Baltimore to try to
rebuild his private practice. He had a difficult time. His stand
on the Bank had left a trail of enemies who tried to block him
at every opportunity. Taney was sick and exhausted. But he remained close to Jackson and several members of the cabinet who
often turned to him for help and advice. Anxious to reward his
trusted friend, and undaunted by the previous senatorial rejec-
tions, Jackson named Taney Chief Justice of the United States
in December, 1835, to replace John Marshall, who had died the
previous July.

Taney won confirmation only after a bitter struggle along party
lines that lasted nearly three months. The Whigs could not forget that he had been responsible for wrecking the Bank of the
United States. They accepted the nomination with very bad
grace. Daniel Webster wrote, "Judge Story thinks the Supreme
Court is *gone*, and I think so too." After the nomination was confirmed by a vote of twenty-nine to fifteen, a leading Whig newspaper remarked that "the pure ermine of the Supreme Court is
sullied by the appointment of that political hack, Roger B. Taney."

It has been well said that "in the drama or novel of redemp-
tion all the sins of an evil past may be forgiven because of a
final act of sacrifice, and so the hero's life may be read in the
light of his ultimate heroism. The reverse was Taney's fate. He

was doomed to have his life read ever in the damning shadow of his final decisions, particularly the Dred Scott case." [1] It is now clear that if it had not been for the Dred Scott case, the legend that Taney was an evil, bigoted, second-rate Chief Justice would never have taken root in American history. For years that one decision was such a blot on his career that it obscured all the valuable contributions he made to American constitutional law.

When Taney succeeded the great Marshall, there were many who feared that the Constitution would be molded to serve the ends of Jacksonian radicalism. It was thought that Taney would destroy the principle of national supremacy for which Marshall had labored for so long against such great odds. But Taney did no such thing. Though he did reassert some state powers, the principle of national supremacy was not destroyed. The Taney Court did reflect the more democratic era by evincing more concern for rights of ordinary individuals and the welfare of the community against private commercial interests. But at the same time, Taney tried to steer a middle course between the nationalism of Marshall and the extreme radicalism of some of the Jacksonians.

During his twenty-eight years as chief justice, Taney wrote nearly three hundred opinions. With few exceptions, he spoke for the Court. In general, he felt that the chief function of the Court was to serve as an arbiter between the various competing interests within the federal system. He also believed firmly in the principle of judicial self-restraint. With the unfortunate exception of the Dred Scott case, this conviction is reflected in his opinions.

It is not surprising that Taney was willing to assign a greater role in the affairs of government to the people and their legislatures. Tied closely to the Jacksonians, he had a deep faith in government by the people. Moreover, as a product of the agrarian culture of the slave-owning South, he distrusted mercantile and

[1] Benjamin W. Palmer, *Marshall and Taney: Statesmen of the Law* (Minneapolis: University of Minnesota Press, 1939), p. 191.

banking interests that sought to accumulate power over others. Two years before becoming chief justice, Taney wrote that "no hands are less worthy to be trusted" with power over persons and property than those of the moneyed corporations.

Taney's honesty, deep conviction, and personal detachment were important assets on the Court. His colleagues came to love and respect him. Many of his political enemies began to regard Taney as a fit successor to Marshall. The Court enjoyed the faith and respect of the nation. Then in 1857 came the Dred Scott case, and the avalanche of criticism seemed to have no end.

In 1857 the controversy over slavery still raged unabated. Compromise after compromise had failed to resolve the differences between North and South. Unfortunately, Taney and some members of the Court, as well as President Buchanan, who had been inaugurated two days before the Dred Scott opinion was announced, were genuinely persuaded that the weight of the Court's opinion would "finally settle" the issue of slavery. Taney, speaking for the Court in the Dred Scott case, held that the Missouri Compromise of 1820, which was designed to ban slavery in the territories, was unconstitutional. Using language that was to provoke violent criticism, Taney further held that no Negro could be a citizen of a state or of the United States. Thus Taney placed the Court squarely behind the slave-holding South in its struggle with the abolitionists.

Taney and his colleagues knew very well what they were doing in the Dred Scott case. "They were attempting to determine national policy, to settle constitutional law in such a way as to prevent the catastrophe which would result if one section of the country attempted to dominate the institutions of the other. In view of the growing power of the North, they regarded their efforts as purely defensive, and not as aids to southern aggression." [1] But it was a monumental error, for the slavery controversy had gone too far to be solved by judicial fiat. Instead of

[1] Swisher, *op. cit.*, pp. 522-523.

"finally settling" the issue, the decision probably hastened the tragic descent to war.

Taney was now a marked man. For years he was to be unmercifully castigated as a diabolical enemy of the Negro, bent on the destruction of all human liberty. Taney was undoubtedly opposed to the wholesale emancipation of the slaves. Yet he certainly was not the beast he was pictured to be. As earlier noted, from his mother he had learned that slavery was morally repugnant and he did favor "voluntary and responsible loosening of the bonds." As an individual citizen he endeavored to better the lot of the slaves in many ways. He freed all the slaves he inherited from his father except those who were too old to take care of themselves. These he helped support by monthly payments from his earnings. Early in his career he had served as legal counsel for a colored peoples' protective association and had defended a Methodist abolitionist accused of inciting a slave rebellion in Maryland. But all this was forgotten in the wave of frenzied, unrestrained criticism. In the Dred Scott case Taney made a mistake that was never really forgiven. "In a critical hour of history, he had made a decision contrary to the best hopes and aspirations of the nation at large."

Taney was a sick, impoverished old man of eighty when the Dred Scott case was decided. Moreover, he was still greatly saddened by the loss of his beloved wife and youngest daughter, both of whom had been swept away by yellow fever in the summer of 1855. He was lonesome and depressed. He had very few close friends. His religious faith alone seemed to sustain him. In truth "there was no sadder figure to be seen in Washington during the years of the Civil War than that of the aged Chief Justice. His form was bent by the weight of years, and his thin, nervous, and deeply-furrowed face was shaded by long, gray locks, and lighted up by large, melancholy eyes that looked wearily out from under shaggy brows, which gave him a weird, wizard-like expression. He had outlived his epoch, and was

shunned and hated by the men of the new time of storm and
struggle for the principles of freedom and nationality." [1]

Yet Taney's most courageous and perhaps greatest opinion was
yet to come. In 1861, in the case of *Ex Parte Merryman*, he delivered his last great opinion and struck the first mighty blow in
federal court history on behalf of individual liberties.

THE CASE

The Merryman case arose during the first anxious days of the
Civil War. With Virginia firmly in the Confederacy, the city of
Washington was in an extremely precarious position from the
beginning of the war. It was essential, therefore, that Maryland
remain loyal to allow the movement of troops through the state
toward the threatened capital. But a goodly number of influential
persons in Baltimore and vicinity were southern sympathizers. In
fact Baltimore was an armed camp determined to keep northern
troops from passing through the state. On April 19, 1861, the
Sixth Massachusetts Militia was stoned by an enraged mob as it
passed through Baltimore. A number of troops were killed or
wounded and a great deal of equipment was lost. That night the
Mayor asked President Lincoln not to permit any more troops to
pass through the city. He stated that "it is not possible for more
soldiers to pass through Baltimore unless they fight their way
at every step."

Other acts of sabotage were committed. Railway bridges leading into Baltimore were burned to prevent further troop movements through the city. Communications were cut off. Supplies
intended for nearby Fort McHenry were seized. Lincoln could
tolerate no more. On April 27, 1861, he directed General Winfield Scott, the commanding general of the army, to suspend the
writ of habeas corpus. The letter to Scott read as follows: "If at

[1] *Ibid.*, pp. 574-575.

any point on or in the vicinity of any military line between the city of Philadelphia and the city of Washington you find resistance which renders it necessary to suspend the writ of habeas corpus for the public safety, you personally or through the officer in command at the point where resistance occurs, are authorized to suspend this writ." [1]

Lincoln's order set a precedent in American history. It marked the first and only time that a President has authorized a military officer to suspend the writ of habeas corpus, which was especially designed to prevent arbitrary arrest or unlawful imprisonment. Moreover, Congress had not authorized the President to issue the order. The Constitution provides that the writ may be suspended in cases of rebellion or invasion, but it does not specify whether Congress or the President may order the suspension. It had long been inferred, however, that only Congress could suspend the writ. Given this background, a conflict with the courts was bound to occur.

It was the arrest of John Merryman that brought about the violent clash between Lincoln and Taney. Merryman, a prominent Baltimore resident of position and property, was president of the state agricultural society and was widely known and respected. A southern sympathizer from the beginning of the war, Merryman soon became an active secessionist. He held a first lieutenant's commission in a rebel cavalry company, which was said to be armed with guns stolen from a federal arsenal. He had been active in inciting actions against northern troops passing through Baltimore. He had supervised the destruction of several bridges between Baltimore and Washington. Moreover, he and several other local citizens had tried to organize military units to oppose the federal forces.

At 2:00 A.M. on May 25, 1861, Merryman was aroused from his bed and arrested by a detachment of troops of the First Pennsylvania Volunteers under the command of Colonel Samuel Yohe,

[1] James D. Richardson, *Messages and Papers of the Presidents*, VI (1899), 18.

who had been ordered to put an end to secessionist activities. Merryman was imprisoned in Fort McHenry, which was commanded by General George Cadwalader. On the same day, through a lawyer who had been permitted to interview him at Fort McHenry, Merryman petitioned Taney for a writ of habeas corpus. At that time Baltimore was part of the circuit over which the Chief Justice presided. As Taney later stated in his opinion in the case, "The petition was presented to me, at Washington under the impression that I would order the prisoner to be brought before me there, but as he was confined in Fort McHenry, in the city of Baltimore, which is in my circuit, I resolved to hear it in the latter city, as obedience to the writ, under such circumstances, would not withdraw General Cadwalader, who had him in charge, from the limits of his military command."

On May 26 Taney issued the writ of habeas corpus directing General Cadwalader to bring Merryman before the circuit court in Baltimore on the following day, so that the reasons for his imprisonment could be examined. The order caused a great deal of excitement. Northerners viewed Taney's speedy issuance of the writ as evidence of his desire to serve the cause of the rebellion. Southern sympathizers, on the other hand, praised Taney's action as a necessary blow for individual liberties against the arrogant assumption of authority by overly zealous Union forces.

On the next morning Baltimore was in turmoil. As one federal officer stated, Baltimore had been sleeping "upon a thin crust right over hell." A number of incidents took place on the streets of the city. Federal troops were jostled by local citizens as they passed in formation. Noisy crowds gathered to shout obscenities at Union troops. At 11:00 A.M. a "gaping mob, pale with anger and hatred," gathered at the court house to witness the outcome of the struggle between their hero, Taney, and General Cadwalader. But the General did not appear in court as he had been ordered the previous day. Instead, he sent a military aide, wearing a full uniform complete with red sash and sword, to read a letter to the court signed by General Cadwalader, pointing out that he had been authorized by the President to suspend the writ of habeas corpus. Therefore, he would not obey the order to bring Merryman before the court. Cadwalader further requested that the case be postponed until the President could be consulted.

Taney was not impressed with Cadwalader's courteous statement. Gravely he noted that Merryman had not been brought before the court as ordered. He therefore promptly issued an attachment for contempt of court against General Cadwalader for refusing to produce Merryman, and made the attachment returnable the next day at twelve o'clock.

On the next day excitement over the case was intense. The court house and the street outside were densely crowded. As he left the house of his son-in-law, then living in Baltimore, to take his seat in circuit, Taney remarked that "it was likely he should be imprisoned in Fort McHenry before night; but that he was going to court to do his duty." [1] Leaning on the arm of his grandson, Taney, sick and bent with age, passed "through a crowd of respectful and sympathizing, but silent spectators" on his way to the court house. Many in the crowd believed that the old man would be imprisoned before the day had ended.

Taney quietly took his seat and called for a return to the writ of attachment. The United States Marshall reported that he had not been allowed to enter Fort McHenry to serve the writ. Taney was thoroughly aroused. He noted that the Marshall had the power to summon a posse to storm the fort and seize Cadwalader but this obviously would be of no avail against the Army's superior forces. Taney, therefore, excused the Marshall from doing more than he had done. In a low, hardly discernible voice Taney then unequivocally stated that Merryman's arrest and detention were unlawful for the following reasons: (1) Under the Constitution, the President cannot suspend the writ of habeas corpus, nor authorize a military aide to do so. (2) A military officer has no right to arrest a person not subject to the rules and articles

[1] Tyler, *op. cit.*, p. 427.

of war. If he does, he must turn the prisoner over immediately to the civil authorities "to be dealt with according to law." Taney stated that he would write out his opinion and send a copy of the entire record of the case to the President.

Taney filed his opinion on June 1. It was a plainly-written, forceful defense of individual freedoms. Relying heavily on both English and American sources, including John Marshall, Taney elaborated upon his statement that the President cannot suspend the writ of habeas corpus. Noting that in England only Parliament can suspend the writ, he argued that under the Constitution the power to authorize suspension in America rested exclusively with Congress. "I can see no ground whatever," wrote Taney, "for supposing that the President, in any emergency or in any state of things, can authorize the suspension of the privileges of the writ of *habeas corpus*, or arrest a citizen, except in the aid of the judicial power. He certainly does not faithfully execute the laws if he takes upon himself legislative power by suspending the writ of *habeas corpus*, and the judicial power also, by arresting and imprisoning a person without due process of law."

Taney then pointed out that the military authority had gone far beyond the mere suspension of the writ of habeas corpus.

It has, by force of arms, thrust aside the judicial authorities and officers to whom the Constitution has confided the power and duty of interpreting and administering the laws, and substituted a military government in its place to be administered and executed by military officers. For at the time these proceedings were had against John Merryman, the District Judge of Maryland, the Commissioner appointed under the act of Congress, the District Attorney, and the Marshall, all resided in the city of Baltimore, a few miles only from the home of the prisoner. . . . If a military officer, or any other person, had reason to believe that the prisoner had committed any offence against the laws of the United States, it was his duty to give information of the fact, and the evidence to support it, to the District Attorney. . . . There was no danger of any obstruction or resistance to the action of the civil authorities, and therefore no reason whatever for the interposition of the militia.

The opinion ends on a melancholy note. Taney stated that Merryman had been deprived of his liberty without due process of law. His arrest constituted an unlawful search and seizure. Moreover, he was denied a speedy trial in an ordinary court of justice. Taney pointed out that these fundamental rights

which Congress itself could not suspend, have been disregarded and suspended, like the writ of *habeas corpus,* by a military order, supported by force of arms. Such is the case now before me, and I can only say that if the authority which the Constitution has confided to the judiciary department and judicial officers may thus upon any pretext or under any circumstances be usurped by the military power at its discretion, the people of the United States are no longer living under a government of laws, but every citizen holds life, liberty, and property at the will and pleasure of the army officer in whose military district he may happen to be found.

Taney stated again that a copy of his opinion would be sent to the President. He concluded, "It will then remain for that high officer, in fulfillment of his constitutional obligation, to 'take care that the laws be faithfully executed,' to determine what measures he will take to cause the civil process to be respected and enforced."

Taney's opinion in the Merryman case was widely discussed throughout the country. As was to be expected, southerners supported the Chief Justice. A few northerners saw some merit in Taney's opinion. The tone of this meager support is revealed well by a letter to the editor of *The New York Times* of June 2, 1861 from a Philadelphian who remarked that it is not well "even in times like these" to disregard the plain provisions of the Constitution. "The people of the North will sustain the Government with heart and hand, but will be zealous of their liberty and personal rights." But such statements were quickly forgotten in the torrent of abuse which was poured out against the aged Chief Justice.

In most of the North, Taney was pictured as another Benedict Arnold. Speakers reminded frenzied crowds that Taney had written the shameful opinion in the Dred Scott case. In a number of communities the Chief Justice was burned in effigy. Typical of the violent press condemnations was an editorial in *The New York Times* of May 30, picturing Taney as "an octogenarian turning back from the grave, on the verge of which he was standing, to strike one last though impotent blow at the existence of a Government he has repeatedly sworn to support. . . . Too feeble to wield the sword against the Constitution, too old and palsied and weak to march in the ranks of rebellion and fight against the Union, he uses the power of his office to serve the cause of the traitors." Long a Taney critic, Horace Greeley remarked in his *New York Daily Tribune* on May 28 that it "would be a happy riddance for the country" if Taney would resign. "But we learn that there is no hope of his doing anything of the kind, for the simple reason that his office is his meat and drink. All well! He cannot live forever, so that the nation is not helplessly delivered over to the mercies of this rebellious judicial autocrat!"

One of Taney's biographers has remarked well that it is now futile "to argue whether the President or the Chief Justice was *right* in the matter, for back of their legal differences were fundamental differences of opinion on matters of public policy. Lincoln preferred to interpret the Constitution so as to avoid the appearance of violating it, but he preferred violating it in one particular to permitting the Union to be destroyed."[1] Taney's sympathies, on the other hand, were unquestionably with the South. He was appalled by the war. To him the maintenance of the Union was not worth the terrible cost. His personal feelings were revealed well in a letter written to former President Franklin Pierce on June 12, 1861. "Peaceful separation of North and South," he wrote, "with free institutions in each section" is far better than Union "under military dictatorship and a reign of terror preceded by a civil war with all its horrors."[2]

[1] Swisher, *op. cit.*, p. 555.
[2] Quoted in Bernard C. Steiner, *Life of Roger Brooke Taney* (Baltimore: Williams and Wilkins, 1922), p. 504.

Lincoln never *directly* answered the Chief Justice. The writ of habeas corpus remained suspended until the war was over. Merryman, however, was later released from Fort McHenry and turned over to civilian authorities. He was subsequently indicted for treason but the case against him was finally dropped. "This was typical of the treatment accorded such cases by the Lincoln administration. When Merryman was no longer capable of harming the Union, Lincoln, who sought no tyranny, gladly washed his hands of the Merryman controversy. But neither the President nor the Chief Justice had a change of heart, and their differences endured."[1]

At the time, Taney's Merryman decision seemed futile indeed. Yet it is now generally agreed that Taney was right in contending that only Congress can suspend the writ of habeas corpus. On this point, the subsequent history of the Court has vindicated him. Only five years after the Merryman decision, in the landmark case of *Ex Parte Milligan*, the Supreme Court sanctioned many of the principles of civil supremacy set forth by Taney in his Merryman opinion. It is ironic indeed that the Milligan opinion was rendered by a Court composed largely of militant Republican Unionists and written by Justice David Davis who had been one of Lincoln's closest friends and most ardent political supporters. "Never did a fearless Judge receive a more swift or more complete vindication." Since the Civil War no attempt has been made by either Congress or the President to suspend the writ of habeas corpus in the United States.

Perhaps, as some have suggested, Taney's opinion in the Merryman case was motivated principally by his sympathy for the South and his hostility toward Lincoln and the war rather than by a passion for civil liberties. Perhaps it is also true that Taney damaged the judiciary by choosing the wrong time and place to challenge Lincoln. Still, we have reason to be grateful for his decision, for it stands as a noble bulwark "against the usurpations

[1] David M. Silver, *Lincoln's Supreme Court* (Urbana: University of Illinois Press, 1956), p. 36.

of military brusqueness and tyranny, and against repressive rule of any kind by executive authority."

But, above all, the Merryman decision reveals Taney's indomitable courage. He had every reason to believe that his action would result in imprisonment. But he refused to be swayed by the public clamor and took the action he firmly believed was right. As a sympathetic biographer has written, Taney's action in the Merryman case "was worthy of the best traditions of the Anglo-Saxon judiciary. There is no sublimer picture in our history than this of the aged Chief Justice—the fires of the Civil War kindling around him, the President usurping the powers of Congress, and Congress itself a seething furnace of sectional animosities—serene and unafraid, while for the third time in his career the storm of partisan fury broke over his devoted head, interposing the shield of the law in the defense of the liberty of the citizen." [1]

Unfortunately, Taney did not live to see his Merryman decision vindicated. A week after the decision was announced Taney wrote to a close friend that he would be glad "to pass the brief remnant of life that may yet be vouchsafed to me in peace with all men, and in the quiet discharge of every-day judicial duties." [2] But this was not to be. Instead, he was abused and condemned to the end.

As he grew older, Taney became more resentful and gloomy. He never forgave Lincoln for disregarding his Merryman opinion. The letters to his friends reveal that he had little hope of better things to come for the country. On August 6, 1863, he wrote to an old Baltimore friend, "The supremacy of the military power over the civil seems to be established; and the public mind has acquiesced in it and sanctioned it." [3] To another friend, a well-known Baltimore lawyer, Taney wrote as follows on March

[1] William E. Mikell, "Roger Brooke Taney," in William D. Lewis *Great American Lawyers* (Philadelphia: John C. Winston, 1908), IV, 188-189.
[2] Tyler, *op. cit.*, p. 431.
[3] *Ibid.*, p. 454.

20, 1864: "I have not only outlived the friends and companions of my early life, but I fear I have outlived the Government of which they were so justly proud, and which has conferred so many blessings upon us. The times are dark with evil omens, and seem to grow darker every day. At my time of life, I cannot expect to live long enough to see these evil days pass away; yet I will indulge the hope that you, who are so much younger, may live to see order and law once more return, and live long to enjoy their blessings." [1]

Taney did not live to see the evil days pass away. On Columbus Day, October 12, 1864, he died at the age of eighty-eight, mourned only by friends and relatives who knew him best. As Chief Justice Warren has written, in death Taney finally found "the peace which had so long eluded him."

[1] *Ibid.*, p. 459.

II

Chief Justice Morrison R. Waite
and *Reynolds* v. *United States*

*Of how a sensitive, hardworking but commonplace and
unspectacular Chief Justice decided that religious belief does
not justify having more than one wife.*

THE MAN

ON THE MORNING OF October 22, 1838, Morrison Remick Waite,
then a young man of twenty-three, arrived by ferry in Maumee
City, Ohio. At that time Maumee City was surrounded by wild
swamplands which made the area "malarious and unhealthful."
To an easterner recently graduated from Yale, the town of less
than eight hundred appeared primitive and desolate. Waite went
immediately to the home of an uncle, a successful merchant who
had previously left Connecticut to settle in Maumee City. That
night he wrote to his father in Lyme, Connecticut, about his trip
west. "I have at last reached this place," he wrote. "It has been
so stormy on the lake for a few days that I have made very slow
progress. I started from Buffalo on Monday last and reached
Cleveland on Thursday—waited at Cleveland for a boat that
would touch at Toledo until yesterday and arrived here this
morning." [1]

[1] This and the following quotation are from the *Waite Papers*, in posses-

Waite was evidently not impressed with his new surroundings. He thought that it might be better to pursue a legal career in various parts of Michigan or Cleveland. He remarked in the letter to his father that the practice of law in Ohio "is about half way between the simplicity of that of Connecticut and the intricacy of that of New York. The fees are not as high as they are in New York and very difficult to collect. I think, however, that I should be content with a location in this place if it were not for the extreme unhealthiness of the climate. There are no good lawyers here and some considerable business with a prospect of more—but although Uncle Horace says it is not unhealthy —yet his face and these faces of the inhabitants tell a different story. I do not think however that it is as sickly here as at Toledo."[1]

Despite these misgivings Waite did begin a legal career in Maumee City, which eventually was to take him to the Supreme Court of the United States. When asked why he had decided to take the trouble of leaving Connecticut for what was then a veritable wilderness, Waite replied that he wanted to make his own way. "Back home, the fact that father is a member of the Supreme Court of Connecticut, would make anything I accomplish in law look like the result of his influence. I want to do it myself. Besides there are too many lawyers in Lyme. They say that the town has produced more lawyers than any town in this country."[2]

The future Chief Justice was born into an old New England family in Lyme on November 29, 1916. The family traced its descent to Thomas Wayte who supposedly was one of the signers of the Death Warrant of King Charles I, executed in 1649. The family name, which was derived from the Old High German *wachten* (to keep watch), was variously spelled Wayte, Wayt,

---

sion of Mr. and Mrs. John B. Waite, Ann Arbor, Michigan and loaned to author, and are used by permission.

[1] *Waite Papers.*

[2] *Morrison Remick Waite Papers.* Manuscript Division, Library of Congress, hereafter cited as *Waite Papers.*

Wayght, or Waitt. But those who migrated to New England eventually settled on Waite. The father of the future Chief Justice was a well-known Connecticut jurist who eventually became chief justice of his state's highest court. Waite's mother was a cultured woman born of an old and distinguished New England family.

Waite attended, as his father had, Bacon Academy and Yale College, which were thirty miles from his home. After graduation in 1837 he read law in his father's office for one year. Upon his arrival in Maumee City he studied law with another transplanted New Englander, Samuel M. Young, and in 1839 he was admitted to the bar. Waite subsequently formed a partnership with Young, and the firm gradually built a sound practice based chiefly on the settlement of insolvent estates and real estate transactions. The practice was by no means confined to the village. Both partners rode circuit, usually on horseback, over almost impassable mud roads and through unbridged streams. During these early years in Maumee City, Waite became known as an honest, thorough, reliable but modest lawyer who could always be counted on to give intelligent advice on important business matters. "He never acquired much reputation as a jury lawyer or spellbinder but he was soon noted for his ability 'to unravel and disclose to a court or jury a fraud even if it lay concealed in the occult mysteries of book-keeping.'" [1]

Two years after arriving in Maumee City, Waite returned to Lyme to marry Amelia Champlin Warner, his second cousin. The marriage won the hearty approval of partner Young, who thought that "there ought to be a wife in the firm and he was not ready to get married himself." In her "Memories" Mrs. Waite recalled that upon their return to Maumee City after the marriage, the young couple furnished a room for a hundred dollars and boarded with Uncle Horace Waite for about eight months. "Then we took a small house and my uncle furnished the house

[1] *Waite Papers.*

comfortably, if not luxuriously. We then, as ever afterward, kept open house." [1]

Despite his reasonably good practice, it soon became apparent to Waite that Toledo rather than Maumee City was to emerge as the important metropolis of northwestern Ohio. In 1850, therefore, Waite moved to Toledo and shortly thereafter formed a new law firm with his youngest brother as partner. The firm prospered and eventually became one of the best-known law firms in the state. It did a great deal of work for the railroad interests.

But unlike his immediate predecessors on the bench—Marshall, Taney, and Chase—Waite did not enter strenuously into the major political controversies of his times. In politics he was first a Whig, and then a Republican with a conservative turn of mind. He generally supported Lincoln's policies. Waite did serve for one term in the Ohio legislature, and in 1862 he made an unsuccessful bid against his own party's candidate for a seat in Congress. Two years later he declined an appointment to the Supreme Court of Ohio, preferring to give his energies to a growing law practice. In 1873 Waite was chosen by both political parties in Toledo as a delegate to the Constitutional Convention. Again he appeared reluctant to leave his law practice, but he felt he could not refuse to serve. "This will run for months," he told his brother. "I can make more money practicing law, but you will have to carry on alone again until I get back. This amending the state constitution is serious business and I feel it is my duty to take part in it." [2] When the convention assembled, Waite was immediately chosen presiding officer.

Although Waite's activities had made him fairly well known in Ohio, he did not come into national prominence until 1871. In that year President Grant named him along with William M. Evarts and Caleb Cushing to represent the United States before

[1] "Memories of Amelia Champlin Waite," p. 3, unfinished manuscript in *Waite Papers.*
[2] *Waite Papers.*

the Geneva Tribunal of Arbitration on the question of the right
of compensation from England for injury to American commerce
by the "Alabama" and other Confederate privateers. It was a
matter of common knowledge that these Confederate cruisers
had operated from British ports during the Civil War, despite
England's proclamation of neutrality. Waite's diligent work on
the commission was overshadowed by the presence of both
Evarts and Cushing who already had national reputations. But
it was Waite who completed the difficult task of unraveling and
writing up the facts of the case. His skillful presentation of the
facts overwhelmed some members of the Geneva Tribunal and
convinced them of the liability of the British government. The
United States was awarded damages of $15,500,000, and the
American delegation came home to be feted and honored by a
grateful people. Toledo gave Waite a rousing reception. It was
generally agreed that Waite's work in Geneva had made him the
equal, if not the peer of his two distinguished colleagues. Yet the
country was taken by surprise when President Grant, in 1874,
named Waite Chief Justice, since he was still unknown to most
of the country and had never held a judicial office nor argued
before the Supreme Court itself.

Waite was by no means Grant's first choice. The President
first quietly offered the job to Roscoe Conkling, a well-known
United States senator and machine politician from New York.
Conkling declined because he had other unfulfilled political
ambitions. Grant's Secretary of State, Hamilton Fish, also declined the appointment. Grant then formally nominated his Attorney General, George H. Williams, but opposition to his nomination was so strong that Grant finally withdrew his name. There
was even more universal dissatisfaction with Grant's next nominee
—the seventy-three-year-old Caleb Cushing of Massachusetts. It
was said of Cushing that he "never allowed principle or conscience to stand in the way of gain; he had not become demoral-
ized, he never was moralized." The hue and cry raised against
Cushing again forced Grant to withdraw the nomination. It was

then that Grant turned to Waite, hoping that his very obscurity would assure his confirmation. An Ohioan later remarked, "It was the queerest appointment that was ever made during Grant's two terms. Everybody was surprised and none more so than men from our own state, where he lived."[1]

Waite was confirmed by the Senate without difficulty, but his appointment aroused little enthusiasm. "The general reaction was that, while better Chief Justices could have been found, the country was lucky to get one who was at least an honest man and a competent lawyer. The Senate hastened to confirm the nomination for fear Grant might change his mind and do worse."[2]

Waite entered upon the duties of his office with less reputation than any of his predecessors. Much of the press referred to him as a mediocre or as a second-rate railroad lawyer. Even friendly newspapers had serious misgivings about his ability to lead the Court through the critical post-Civil War period. The members of the Court themselves exhibited a marked coolness toward their new chief upon his arrival in Washington. Some regarded him as an interloper. Others who had aspired to the top position resented his appointment.

Justice Miller, who had himself felt justly entitled to lead the Court, described Waite as a "pleasant but mediocre" judge. This tone of disparagement persisted throughout Waite's career on the Court. In 1875 Justice Miller remarked that he could not "make a silk purse out of a sow's ear. I can't make a great Chief Justice out of a small man."[3] And in 1879 Miller wrote that his chief "is much more anxious to be popular as an amiable, kind hearted man (which he is) than as the dignified and capable head of the greatest court the world ever knew. Of what is due

[1] *Toledo Blade,* January 24, 1885, quoted by Mrs. Mathew S. Morgan in "How Morrison R. Waite Came to be Nominated Chief Justice of the United States," *Northwest Ohio Quarterly,* XXIII (Summer, 1951), 141.

[2] Kenneth B. Umbreit, *Our Eleven Chief Justices* (New York: Harper and Bros., 1938), p. 315.

[3] Charles Fairman, *Mr. Justice Miller and the Supreme Court 1862-1890* (Cambridge: Harvard University Press, 1939), p. 373.

to that court, and what is becoming its character, he has no conception." [1]

It is now clear that Justice Miller's own disappointment in being passed over for the chief justiceship affected his judgment of Waite. Miller's biographer has noted well that Waite's "unaffected kindliness was a most useful lubricant in a Court which included some very strong personalities, and in other ways he proved to be a more considerable person than his associates at first recognized." [2] And even Miller was to remark upon the death of Waite that "the oldest members of this Court know of no one who was better fitted to discharge the administrative duties of the office of its Chief Justice, or who did so with more acceptability to his associates and to the public at large." [3]

Throughout his fourteen years on the Court Waite was able to lessen frictions, allay jealousies, and keep strong-minded and intellectually superior men like Justices Samuel F. Miller, Stephen J. Field, and Joseph P. Bradley working together in a common cause. In fact, he emerged as one of the Court's most successful administrators. Waite's success was not attained because he was brilliant or showy. He had neither the genius nor the term of service of his illustrious predecessors, Taney and Marshall. But he was a kindly, modest man of integrity with an orderly mind and a high sense of devotion to duty. He could work twelve hours a day for weeks on end and still participate in the demanding social life of Washington. He was a careful, courteous and generous man. He gave all of himself to the work of the Court. Justice Blatchford once wrote to Waite that "my path as been strewn with flowers since I came here [on the Court], thanks to your kind and generous aid." In 1886 Justice Blatchford wrote to Waite that "your brethren alone, in the intimacy of the conference room . . . know the skill, the patience, the uniform good

[1] *Ibid.*, p. 409.
[2] *Ibid.*, p. 373.
[3] "Memorial Before Association of Bar of City of New York," March 31, 1888, *Waite Papers.*

temper, and the high sense of the dignity of the Court which have marked the discharge of your duties." [1] Many other warm, friendly letters to Waite from the other members of the Court found in his papers reveal a high regard for the work of the Chief Justice.

Waite's singular devotion to the duties of his office is revealed well by his total lack of political ambition. His predecessor, Chief Justice Chase, had never been able to forget his presidential ambitions. In fact, he viewed the Chief Justiceship largely as a springboard to the Presidency. Other members of the Court appeared to be biding their time for the "call" to political prominence. Such a thought was intolerable to Waite. In 1875 Waite was mentioned in a number of newspapers as a possible candidate for President. A number of friends urged him to declare himself a candidate. The rumor was spread that he might run. But a letter to one of his boosters quickly settled the matter. "The office of Chief Justice," wrote Waite, "has come down to me covered with honor. When I accepted it, my duty was not to make it a stepping-stone to something else, but to preserve its purity and make my own name as honorable, if possible, as that of my predecessors. . . . Can I with propriety permit my name to be used for the formation of political combinations? If I do, can I remain at all times and in all cases an unbiased judge in the estimation of the people? If I am not, shall not I degrade my office?" And later he wrote that "no Chief Justice of my court can be a candidate for the Presidency without removing at least one stone from the foundation that upholds the government." [2]

Waite was always ready to do more than his share of the Court's work. He always took over the unfinished tasks of an ill colleague graciously and cheerfully. He gave unstintingly of his time to colleagues who sought advice. During his tenure he wrote over a thousand opinions. Many of these, the originals of which are still preserved in his own handwriting, were the result of

[1] *Waite Papers.*
[2] *Ibid.*

grueling, painstaking toil. His opinions are, as Justice Bradley
once wrote, "terse, clear, and to the point." They furnish a "silent
rebuke to the rambling treatises to which we are obliged to listen." In addition, Waite's opinions, although sometimes clumsy
and opaque, are characterized by common sense, moderation, and
candor. In short, Waite was a competent but completely unspectacular man. He had the touch of the soil about him—he was
commonplace. He was not a dramatic figure. Justice Frankfurter
has said that Waite lacked style and "the grand manner. The stuff
of the artist was not in him." He "evidently was one of those able
judges whose 'instinct for the jugular' is incapable of artistic execution." [1] Waite's opinions also make dry reading, in part, because he believed firmly that the Court was not to enlarge its
authority at the expense of the legislature. Thus, Waite stuck to
the specifics of each case. He was unwilling to embellish or em-
broider in order to enlarge the Court's authority. He was no
phrase-maker. He was satisfied to be a lawyer—a craftsman who
adhered to the "conventional canons of judicial review." Moreover, it must be remembered that Waite had no other personal
ambition. He did not try to attract attention or become "popular."
And in part, "Waite's failure to gain a great reputation is due to
the fact that the Court functioned too successfully during his term
of office. Institutions which function competently, efficiently and
quietly do not often attract the public eye." [2]

Just after he had been named Chief Justice, a resident of
Toledo, Ohio, wrote to Waite requesting his autograph and noted
that "the Supreme Court is about all that is left for us to revere,
as citizens—every other high place in the land can be bought or
sold—so it seems. God, in His infinite mercy grant, that never a
stain may soil the purity of *your* judicial ermine." [3] After Waite's
death fourteen years later, a letter to Mrs. Waite dated March 25,

[1] Felix Frankfurter, *The Commerce Clause Under Marshall, Taney and
Waite* (Chapel Hill: University of North Carolina Press, 1937), pp. 79-80.
[2] Umbreit, *op. cit.*, p. 300.
[3] *Waite Papers.*

1888, from San Antonio, Texas, offered condolences and, like many others, stated that the late Chief Justice had "honored the exalted position which he occupied. He has lain aside the judicial ermine unspotted and unblemished."[1] But though Chief Justice Waite won great respect for his judicial service in an age marked by unbelievable graft and dishonesty, he has never been regarded as one of the glittering stars of the Supreme Court. His name is unknown to the great mass of men.

It has been well said that Waite was an ordinary man, but he "possessed to an extraordinary degree the capacity for his office." Long a railroad lawyer, Waite was able to transcend conscious or unconscious sympathy for the side he had once served. "He did not confine the Constitution within the limits of his own experience, nor did he read merely his own mind to discover the powers that may be exercised by a great nation. The disciplined and disinterested lawyer in him transcended the bounds of the environment within which he moved and the views of the clients whom he served at the bar."[2]

In an age when public virtue was by no means commonplace, Waite remained a poor man devoted to the public good. The year before he went to the Court, the income from his law practice was over $25,000. The salary of a Chief Justice at that time was $10,000. This was inadequate since Waite had to pay for entertainment and bear all the other expenses connected with his position. Throughout his tenure on the Court Waite borrowed money from his former law partner in Toledo and other friends. During his last years on the Court his letters show that he was constantly worried about meeting his expenses. Yet he was always ready to give a "mite" to some charity, an old friend, or even a complete stranger like the practicing physician in Ohio who asked for a loan of $20.00 "for treatment of an illness."

When Waite died, he left only his home in Washington, which was worth $25,000, to his widow and unmarried daughter.

[1] *Ibid.*
[2] Frankfurter, *op. cit.*, p. 111.

Friends in New York and other parts of the country subsequently
raised two funds for the support of his family. Yet, like Justice
Miller, throughout his judicial career Waite refused to participate in any financial scheme which might have affected his impartiality on the Court.

It is certainly true that Waite's imagination "was never ignited
by the spark of genius." But this fact should not dim the very real
accomplishments of a plain, honest man of few pretenses who
labored incessantly to clear his crowded docket of its new and
unfamiliar problems. Waite's most famous decision was *Munn* v.
Illinois where he helped pave the way toward the modern social
service state by holding that private property may be regulated
by a state "when used in a manner to make it of public conse-
quence and affect the community at large." In this sense Waite
was the forerunner of the liberal group of justices who finally
gave their blessing to the New Deal.

Despite Waite's vague and somewhat ambivalent liberal opinion in the Munn case, he was essentially a conservative. In matters of individual rights versus the established government, Waite
usually resolved all doubt in favor of the government. In short,
he was more concerned with safeguarding the general public interest than with individual rights. Of course, in Waite's time there
were few civil rights cases. The most important of these during
his tenure was *Reynolds* v. *United States,* where the Court considered, *for the first time,* the meaning of the First Amendment
in the field of religion. Whether right or wrong, the fundamentals
of Waite's reasoning in that case endure to this day.

The Case

In an earlier day the Church of Jesus Christ of Latter-Day
Saints, commonly called the Mormon Church, publicly advocated
polygamy as a religious tenet. A small number of these Mormons
engaged in plural marriage, particularly after their migration to

Utah. According to the doctrines of the Church only those members who were considered fit both financially and morally could
practice polygamy.

With the increase of non-Mormons in the Utah territory, pressure began to build in Congress for legislation which would put
an end to the "immoral practice" of plural marriages. Legislation
designed to outlaw polygamy was first introduced in Congress in
1860 by Representative J. S. Morrill of Vermont. In 1862 Congress
finally passed the Morrill "anti-bigamy bill," which made polygamy a crime in the territories. The Morrill Act, however, proved
to be ineffective. Convictions were difficult to obtain because it
was worded in such a way that there could be no interference
with the dictates of conscience. The Mormons regarded the law
as clearly unconstitutional. As a result, it was all but impossible
to gather testimony and obtain witnesses for prosecutions under
the Act. Wives refused to testify against accused husbands. Witnesses were spirited away at crucial points in a case. Mormon
juries refused to convict polygamists under the law. Moreover,
Americans were, in general, too deeply involved in the problems
of the Civil War and Reconstruction to concern themselves very
much with a minority group like the Mormons. But with the
end of the war and problems of Reconstruction at least partially
resolved, the "Mormon Question" became a "national preoccupa-
tion, filling the vacuum left by the victory over slavery." A fierce
and relentless crusade to wipe out the "peculiar institution" of
polygamy was launched.

George Reynolds, one of the leading officials of the Mormon
Church, was a believer in plural marriages. He served as secretary
to Brigham Young, President of the Church, who at one time
had twenty-seven wives. Reynolds had only two wives, but in
1874 he was charged with and convicted of bigamy in violation
of the Morrill Act. Although there is no proof, it appears that
Reynolds' trial resulted from an informal agreement between
church leaders and federal officials to test the constitutionality of
the antibigamy law. Reynolds' conviction was set aside by the

Utah territorial supreme court for technical reasons. But he was tried again, convicted and sentenced to two years' imprisonment at hard labor and fined $500. The second conviction was sustained by the territorial supreme court. Reynolds then appealed to the Supreme Court of the United States.

Before the Court, Reynolds, who was said to suffer from severe migraine headaches caused by anxieties in trying to make plural marriages successful in a hostile environment, argued that his marriage behavior was justified by his religious belief. Since polygamy was a part of his religion, the Morrill Act violated his free exercise of religion under the First Amendment. But the Supreme Court in an opinion delivered by Chief Justice Waite did not agree. After disposing of several technical points, Waite noted that Congress cannot pass a law which prohibits the free exercise of religion. But since "religion" is not defined precisely in the Constitution, Waite cited Jefferson to show that by the freedom of religion clause of the First Amendment, "Congress was deprived of all legislative power over mere opinion, but was left free to reach actions which were in violation of social duties or subversive of good order."

Waite then launched into a scathing indictment of plural marriages. He pointed out that "polygamy has always been odious among the northern and western nations of Europe, and until the establishment of the Mormon Church, was almost exclusively a feature of the life of Asiatic and African people." He pointed out that from the "earliest history of England polygamy has been treated as an offence against society, and that the death penalty was inflicted for the crime in both England and Wales under James I. Polygamy was illegal in all the American colonies. Every state in the Union made polygamy a punishable offence." Hence, Waite concluded that "in the face of all this evidence, it is impossible to believe that the constitutional guaranty of religious freedom was intended to prohibit legislation in respect to this most important feature of social life."

Waite held that the Morrill Act was constitutional and valid.

This being so, the only question which remains is, whether those who make polygamy a part of their religion are excepted from the operation of the statute. If they are, then those who do not make polygamy a part of their religious belief may be found guilty and punished, while those who do, must be acquitted and go free. This would be introducing a new element into criminal law. Laws are made for the government of actions, and while they cannot interfere with mere religious belief and opinions, they may with practices. Suppose one believed that human sacrifices were a necessary part of religious worship, would it be seriously contended that the civil government under which he lived could not interfere to prevent a sacrifice? Or if a wife religiously believed it was her duty to burn herself upon the funeral pile of her dead husband, would it be beyond the power of the civil government to prevent her from carrying her belief into practice? So here, as a law of the organization of society under the exclusive dominion of the United States, it is provided that plural marriages shall not be allowed. Can a man excuse his practices to the contrary because of his religious belief? To permit this would be to make the professed doctrines of religious belief superior to the law of the land, and in effect to permit every citizen to become a law unto himself. Government could exist only in name under such circumstances.

Waite concluded that freedom of religion pertains to belief rather than action. Reynolds could believe that he should have more than one wife and go unpunished. But when he actually practiced polygamy he could be punished. Waite's decision made it clear that freedom of religion, like other freedoms, is not absolute or unlimited. Actions in the name of religious liberty that offend public morals cannot be condoned.

The Reynolds decision set the stage for an unrelenting assault upon the Mormons. In 1880 President Hayes declared in his message to Congress that the people of the United States had a duty "to suppress polygamy where it now exists in one territory and prevent its extension." The next year President Arthur asked for legislation to abolish "this odious crime." Congress acted quickly. During the 1880's stringent legislation was passed which, among other things, outlawed the Mormon militia, disfranchised Mormons, and confiscated all church land except that held for bona fide church purposes. This legislation was upheld by the Supreme Court, which followed Waite's lead in denouncing polygamy.

The pressure against the Mormons soon became too great. Hundreds of Mormons were prosecuted under the new legislation. The taking of church property seriously weakened the economic strength of the Church. Many Mormons themselves began to agitate for the abandonment of polygamy. Finally, in 1890, these pressures as well as Utah's desire for statehood brought an end to polygamy. In that year the President of the Mormon Church issued a manifesto declaring as follows:

Inasmuch as laws have been enacted by Congress forbidding plural marriages, which laws have been pronounced constitutional by the court of last resort, I hereby declare my intention to submit to those laws and to use my influence with the members of the Church over which I preside to have them do likewise. . . .

There is nothing in my teachings to the Church or in those of my associates, during the time specified, which can be reasonably construed to inculcate or encourage polygamy; and when an Elder of the Church has used language which appeared to convey any such teaching, he has been promptly reproved. And I now publicly declare that my advice to the Latter-day Saints is to refrain from contracting any marriage forbidden by the law of the land.[1]

In 1894 Congress passed an enabling act providing for the admission of Utah to the Union on condition that the state constitution contain a provision prohibiting "polygamous or plural marriages" forever. This condition was met and Utah was admitted to the Union in 1896. Today polygamy has been virtually eliminated in the United States. Only a handful of members of a Mormon sect known as the Fundamentalists still attempt to practice polygamy.

[1] Quoted in William Mulder and Russel A. Mortensen (eds.), *Among the Mormons* (New York: A. A. Knopf, 1958), pp. 416-417.

The tenacity of Waite's opinion in the Reynolds case, which undoubtedly has had the support of the overwhelming majority of Americans, is shown clearly by the Supreme Court's decision in *Cleveland* v. *United States*, rendered in 1946. There Justice William O. Douglas, speaking for the Court over the lone dissent of Justice Frank Murphy, held that it is a violation of the Mann Act for a man to transport a woman across state lines for the purpose of making her his plural wife or cohabiting with her as such. The Mann Act makes it unlawful to transport in interstate commerce "any woman or girl for the purpose of prostitution or debauchery, or for any other immoral purpose." Relying on Waite's denunciation of polygamy as odious to the western nations, Douglas reasoned that polygamous practices were covered by the phrase "any other immoral purpose" since the "establishment or maintenance of polygamous households is a notorious example of promiscuity."

III

Justice John M. Harlan
and *Plessy* v. *Ferguson*

*Of how a former Democrat and slave-holder from Kentucky,
who once denounced Lincoln's Emancipation Proclamation,
stood alone against the judicial sanction of segregation.*

THE MAN

NO AMERICAN NEGRO living in the early years of the Civil War
would have dreamed that John Marshall Harlan would one day
become an ardent defender of Negro rights. Not only was Harlan
a southerner but, in addition, both he and his father had owned
slaves. Moreover, Harlan had been a stanch Whig who opposed
Lincoln's proclamation to free the slaves. Yet, as a Supreme Court
justice, Harlan emerged as a dedicated champion of Negro rights.
The story of his conversion to the Negro cause is an intriguing
one indeed.

Justice Harlan looked like a man who belonged on the Supreme Court despite the fact that he was a careless dresser.
Dubbed the "Kentucky giant" because he was over six feet tall,
Harlan was a magnificent figure of a man. He had broad, massive shoulders and long arms. He walked as if the whole world
belonged to him. "A broad dome of a forehead topped his florid
face; his deep set eyes burned with a smouldering fire beneath

This chapter appeared as an article in *The Quarterly Review of Higher
Education among Negroes*, XXX, No. 1 (January, 1962). Reprinted by permission.

their shaggy brows. His long black frock coat was usually rumpled, his high hat was battered, his collar flared wide at the corners, and his shirt escaped from under his chin in uncontrolled abandon. But his bearing was regal, and wherever he went he caught the admiring eye. His voice, often in startling contrast to the low, studied voices of his associates when in Court rang like a great gong." [1]

Harlan was born on a farm in Boyle County, Kentucky in 1833. He was named John Marshall because his father, James Harlan, was an ardent admirer of the great Chief Justice. Moreover, he wanted his newborn, redheaded son to become a lawyer like himself. James Harlan was a successful Whig politician who exerted a strong influence on his son in many other ways. A devout Presbyterian, he transmitted to his son his deep religious faith and his inborn hatred for the institution of slavery. Until the Civil War there were ten to twelve inherited slaves in the Harlan household, but James Harlan always disliked the evils that came with slavery. He was not an abolitionist because he felt that forced emancipation of the slaves would violate the right of self-government and the property rights of American citizens. But he accepted the responsibility for the welfare of the slaves, always doing the best he could for them. He treated them kindly, and educated and freed those of unusual ability. Legend has it that one of the freed men went to California in the gold rush of 1849 and struck it rich.

In 1835 the family left the old stone farmhouse and moved to Harrodsburg. Five years later James Harlan piled his household goods on the family wagon and moved to Frankfort, the state capital, where he was to serve as Secretary of State for Kentucky. At various times James Harlan was also a member of Congress, State Attorney General, and a federal district attorney. He was a personal friend of the leading Whig politicians of the day, including Henry Clay. Young Harlan thus grew up in a household

1 Winfield Shiras, *Justice George Shiras, Jr. of Pittsburgh* (Pittsburgh: University of Pittsburgh Press, 1953), p. 105.

where practical political problems were discussed constantly. He was only eleven years of age when he began to take a real interest in the political movements of the period.

James Harlan was able to provide his children—six boys and three girls—with a better than average education. John Marshall attended private schools and was later graduated with honors from Centre College, a small but strict Presbyterian institution, located only a few miles from the old Harlan farm. He then began to study law at Transylvania University in Lexington. At that time Transylvania was highly regarded and was known as the "Harvard of the West." Harlan completed his law studies in 1852 and was admitted to the bar during the next year. He was now only twenty years of age. Life was indeed promising.

Harlan returned to Frankfort and joined his father and older brother in the general practice of law. As a stanch young Whig, he plunged into politics and was elected city attorney in 1854. Two years later he was reelected. In December, 1856, Harlan married Malvina Shanklin whom he had met in Evansville, Indiana, while visiting his older married sister. In accordance with the custom of the times, the young couple went to live with the elder Harlans. In her memoirs, the new Mrs. Harlan, who had grown up in a family which was strongly opposed to slavery, described her new home in Frankfort.

The town house of my husband's family was an old-fashioned frame mansion, with spacious rooms, standing at one corner of an unusually wide and deep lot. . . . In the end of the long ell extending from one side of the town house, and in the cabins at the back of the lot, lived the slaves, who had been inherited from both sides of the Harlan family. There were almost as many slaves as there were members of 'the family' (about a dozen). . . . The close sympathy existing between the slaves and their Master or Mistress was a source of great wonder to me as a descendant of the Puritans, and I was often obliged to admit to myself that my former views of the awful Institution of Slavery would have to be somewhat modified.[1]

[1] Alan F. Westin, "The First Justice Harlan: A Self-Portrait from His

When Harlan entered politics, he was confronted immediately with the smoldering conflict over slavery and the rights of Negroes. The Negro issue was one that Harlan could not escape. It was to haunt him throughout his political career, for it was an issue that saturated the United States "from border to border, and past, into the virgin lands of the unexplored West. Men who were Whigs or Democrats, merchants, farmers, or professionals, laborers or ne'er-do-wells—these men were suddenly separated by a gap that transcended all others. Were they for slavery or against it?"

The slavery question destroyed the Whig Party. The Whigs had played an important role in American politics for twenty years. Formed in opposition to the autocratic methods of Andrew Jackson, whom they had dubbed King Andrew the First, the Whigs had sent two military heroes—Henry Harrison and Zachary Taylor—to the White House. But the slavery issue split the party in two. The southern Whigs joined hands with the pro-slavery Democrats, while the Northern Whigs merged with abolitionists and other groups to form the Republican Party. The Kentucky Whigs tried to side-step the slavery issue by joining the newly-formed American Party, which sought to exploit the hostile feelings against newly-arrived immigrants from Europe. Behind the American Party was a secret organization called the Know-Nothing Society whose motto was "put none but Americans on guard." The Know Nothings tried to combat the "alien menace" by seeking to exclude foreigners and Roman Catholics from all public offices. Like most other good Kentucky Whigs, John Harlan joined the Know-Nothing Society. He later himself related how he came to join the organization. "I was very uncomfortable when the oath [to vote only for American-born Protestants] was administered," he wrote.

My conscience, for a time, rebelled against it. For a moment I had the thought of retiring; for while I was intense, as I still am, in my

Private Papers," *Kentucky Law Journal*, Spring, 1958, p. 331. Reprinted by permission.

Protestantism, I did not relish the idea of proscribing anyone on account of his religion. But looking around the room in which the initiation occurred, I observed that the old Whig leaders of the city, including my father, were present, and I had not the boldness to repudiate the organization. So I remained in it, upon the idea that, *all things* considered, it was best for *any* organization to control public affairs than to have the Democratic party in power. . . . I knew at that time that the Democratic party in fact pandered to and courted foreign influence, in order to get the votes of foreigners, and that in many parts of the country the leaders of that party were in league with Catholic priests—the latter, by their machinations with Democratic leaders, obtaining favors for their church (as in New York City), which were not accorded to Protestant churches. So I became reconciled to remaining in the Know-Nothing Society, notwithstanding its direct attack on the Catholic Church.[1]

Throughout the 1850's John Harlan stumped the state on behalf of the American Party, delivering anti-foreign and anti-Catholic but mildly pro-slavery speeches. He became one of Kentucky's best-known citizens, and in 1858 was elected judge of Franklin County (Frankfort) on the American Party ticket. But the American Party was on its way out. In 1856 it collapsed in the national elections. The ex-Whigs were again in search of a party. In 1860 they cast their lot with John Bell and the Constitutional Union Party, which straddled the slavery issue and sought to preserve the Union through compromise and conciliation. John Harlan was chosen as an elector and campaigned for the party in Kentucky, where Bell supporters hauled and clanged a two-thousand-pound bell all over the state to arouse supporters. The "bell-ringers" won Kentucky but they carried only two other states—Tennessee and Virginia. Lincoln had won only 1,400 votes in Kentucky; but he had been elected President. When the Confederates fired on Fort Sumter in April 1861, the choice could no longer be postponed. Like so many others, John Harlan had to choose between slavery-with-secession and the Union. Harlan

[1] *Ibid.,* pp. 332-333.

had never advocated general emancipation for the Negro. In fact, he had supported and espoused the institution of slavery. But though he wanted slavery, he wanted the Union even more.

When war came, Harlan strove valiantly to prevent Kentucky's secession from the Union. Then he recruited an infantry regiment—the Tenth Kentucky Volunteers—and left his wife and two small children for service as a colonel in Kentucky, Mississippi, and Tennessee. Through the sufferings and privations of war, Harlan came to know intimately many men of all classes and creeds for the first time. He learned to appreciate the problems of men who had been less fortunate than he. Some of his previous antagonism toward Catholics and immigrants melted away. The Army gave Harlan an opportunity to develop sympathy for the common man which was to last a lifetime.

In 1863 the sudden death of his father forced Harlan to retire from the army since he alone could take charge of unsettled business affairs and support his mother and family. He returned home and plunged immediately into politics. He ran for state Attorney General on the Constitutional Union Party ticket and won a resounding victory. In his campaign for the office Harlan attacked Lincoln's Emancipation Proclamation, arguing that the Civil War was being fought to preserve the Union and not to eradicate slavery. In the presidential campaign of 1864 he sounded the same note in campaigning vigorously for General George B. McClellan against Lincoln. In a campaign speech in Indiana, Harlan attacked Lincoln for assuming unconstitutional powers and for waging war chiefly to free the slaves rather than to preserve the Union. Harlan asked why the North had decided to fight. "It was to maintain the Union, and the Constitution which was the only bond of that Union. It was for the high and noble purpose of asserting the binding authority of our laws over every part of this land. It was not for the purpose of giving freedom to the Negro. . . . Mr. Lincoln has in disregard of the then declared purpose of the nation changed and perverted the character of the war. He is warring chiefly for the freedom of the African race.

He will not be content with simply re-establishing the authority of the Constitution and restoring the union." [1]

For the next few years Harlan continued to denounce the Republicans. He opposed the Thirteenth Amendment, which abolished slavery, because he felt it invaded states' rights and violated promises made to Kentucky slave-holders. But gradually Harlan drifted into the ranks of the Republican Party. There were many reasons for his conversion. By 1868 he had left Frankfort for the more liberal environment of Louisville to practice law with Benjamin Bristow, a leading Republican politician. Many of Harlan's new clients were Republicans whose views won his respect. Moreover, politically Harlan simply had no place else to go. His middle-of-the-road Constitutional Union Party was dead. He could not stomach the secession beliefs of the Democrats. So in 1868 Harlan found himself campaigning for the Republican presidential candidate, Ulysses S. Grant. Harlan's conversion was complete. He took over the leadership of the struggling Republicans in his state. He ran for governor twice and, in defeat, laid the ground for an emerging party structure.

Of course Harlan's conversion to Republicanism forced him to reconsider his position on slavery and the Negro. This he did with his usual forthrightness and without apology. Slavery was now ended. "Perhaps grudgingly at first, perhaps with the feeling that too much had been done too fast," Harlan began to accept the results of the war. His new-found conviction was strengthened and reinforced by the wave of violence and lawlessness that swept Kentucky and the South after 1868. The floggings, rapes, lynchings and murders by lawless bands horrified Harlan. As a man committed deeply to law and order, he knew that violence as espoused by groups such as the Ku Klux Klan offered no solution. And so Harlan began to give his whole-

---

[1] Alan F. Westin, "John Marshall Harlan and the Constitutional Rights of Negroes," *Yale Law Journal*, LXVI (April, 1957), 651. Reprinted by permission.

hearted support to the cause of Negro rights. He proclaimed publicly that his pro-slavery views had been completely wrong. Thus he declared in a campaign address that "the most perfect despotism that ever existed on this earth was the institution of African slavery. It was an enemy to free speech; it was an enemy to good government; it was an enemy to a free press. . . . I rejoice that it is gone; I rejoice that the Sun of American Liberty does not this day shine upon a single human slave upon this continent; I rejoice that these human beings are now in possession of freedom, and that that freedom is secured to them in the fundamental law of the land, beyond the control of the state. . . . Let it be said that I am right rather than consistent." [1]

In 1876 Harlan headed the Kentucky delegation to the Republican National Convention in Cincinnati. The delegation was pledged to vote for the state's favorite son, Benjamin R. Bristow, Harlan's law partner, who was then in Washington as Secretary of the Treasury. But when it became clear to Harlan that Bristow could not win the nomination, he took the entire delegation into the Rutherford B. Hayes camp at the crucial moment. As a result, Hayes won the nomination and subsequently became President after a bitter, hotly disputed election. Harlan had made a deep impression on the new President. Not only was Hayes grateful for Harlan's support, but he admired also Harlan's abilities as a lawyer and a statesman. In 1877, when Justice David Davis resigned from the Supreme Court to accept a seat in the United States Senate, Harlan was appointed to fill the vacancy.

Harlan served on the Court until his death in October, 1911—a period of over thirty-three years. Only Justice Field and Chief Justice Marshall exceeded his long tenure on the Court. During those years Harlan was a veritable work horse. He wrote over eight hundred majority and concurring opinions and delivered over three hundred dissents. He is undoubtedly the Court's "greatest dissenter," for his forceful dissenting opinions have, in many

[1] *Ibid.*, pp. 659-660.

instances, stood the test of time and been adopted by later generations.

Harlan's approach to law was simple and direct. He had no patience with refined, subtle distinctions. He believed firmly that the interpretation of the Constitution should be based on common sense. "His opinions are supported by abundant authority, but make no vain display of learning and of their meaning there is no room for doubt." Harlan was not a compromiser. A man of strength and imagination, he had the courage to stand alone when convinced that he was right. He believed strongly that the Supreme Court had a special duty to defend the liberties of all Americans. Above all, Harlan was a humanitarian who wanted "to see to it that the weak were not overmastered by the strong." Nowhere is his creed more evident than in his attitude toward the Negro. He was on the side of Negro civil rights in *every* case that came before the Court even when he was forced to stand alone in dissent. Seldom has the American Negro had such a courageous judicial champion.

Of all his civil rights opinions, Harlan's solitary dissent in *Plessy* v. *Ferguson* is the most powerful and dramatic. It stands today as a classic in the literature of American civil rights.

THE CASE

At the end of the Civil War it seemed that the Negro had finally won his freedom. But the war was hardly over before the South began to fight bitterly to turn back the tide running toward full emancipation of the Negro. Gradually he was relegated to a position of complete inferiority not very different from his pre-Civil War slave status. This was accomplished, in part, by a host of state laws and local ordinances, enacted principally after 1880, that separated whites and Negroes in every possible area of activity. Negroes were segregated in trains, buses, steamboats, schools, hospitals, and places of amusement. Drinking fountains, elevators, stairways, doorways, waiting rooms, parks, toilets, pay windows, and even churches were all made separate for whites and Negroes. Some communities went to ridiculous ends indeed to guarantee segregation everywhere. New Orleans, for example, segregated white and Negro prostitutes. In Atlanta, Georgia, Negroes and whites were not allowed to visit the local zoo at the same time. And Oklahoma required that telephone companies maintain separate booths for white and colored patrons. In effect, a separate world designed "to keep the Negro in his place" and insure white supremacy was created. A few sensible people both North and South protested this madness, but with no effect. In 1896 the Supreme Court formally approved the pattern of segregation established in the South in the famous case of *Plessy* v. *Ferguson.*

The Plessy case grew out of a Louisiana law passed in 1890 that required railroads to provide "separate but equal" accommodations for white and colored passengers. On June 2, 1892, Homer Plessy, who was only one-eighth Negro and appeared to be white, boarded a train in New Orleans and took a vacant seat in a coach reserved for white persons. The conductor ordered Plessy to move to a coach for colored passengers, but he refused. With the aid of a police officer Plessy was thereupon forcibly ejected from the train, locked up in the New Orleans jail, and taken before a Judge Ferguson to answer a charge of violating the Louisiana Law. In affirming his conviction, the Supreme Court of Louisiana upheld the state statute. Plessy then appealed to the Supreme Court.

Two southerners—Harlan and Justice Edward D. White of Louisiana—sat on the Court when the Plessy case was decided. The other justices came from Maine, Connecticut, Massachusetts, Michigan, Pennsylvania, and New York. Justice David Brewer who was born in Asia but had spent his early youth in Connecticut, did not participate in the decision. The majority opinion, written by Justice Henry B. Brown, Michigan's first Supreme Court justice, was supported by all the participating justices except Harlan. Plessy's lawyers had argued that the Louisiana segregation law was unconstitutional under both the Thirteenth Amendment of the Constitution, abolishing slavery, and the equal protection clause of the Fourteenth Amendment. Justice Brown quickly brushed aside these arguments with the assertion that segregation was lawful as long as equal facilities were provided for both races. Plessy's argument that segregation branded the Negro with a badge of inferiority was curtly dismissed by Justice Brown with the incredible assertion that "if this is so, it is not by reason of anything found in the act, but solely because the colored race chooses to put that construction upon it."

Harlan's solitary dissenting opinion has been justly characterized as one of the most vigorous and forthright dissents in Supreme Court history. The former slave-owner from Kentucky took his stand without apology in eloquent, bristling language which must have caused at least some twinge of guilt among his colleagues from the North. He noted that the Thirteenth and Fourteenth Amendments were designed to end discrimination based on color. Segregation, to Harlan, *was* discrimination against the Negro. He remarked,

everyone knows that the statute in question had its origin in the purpose, not so much to exclude white persons from railroad cars occupied by blacks, as to exclude colored people from coaches occupied by or assigned to white persons. Railroad corporations of Louisiana did not make discrimination among whites in the matter of accomodation for travellers. The thing to accomplish was, under the guise of giving equal accomodation for whites and blacks, to compel the latter to keep to themselves while traveling in railroad passenger coaches. No one would be so wanting in candor as to assert the contrary. The fundamental objection, therefore, to the statute is that it interferes with the personal freedom of citizens. . . . If a white man and a black man choose to occupy the same public conveyance on a public highway, it is their right to do so, and no government, proceeding alone on grounds of race, can prevent it without infringing the personal liberty of each.

Harlan went on to say, in a statement that has been widely quoted in recent years, that under the Constitution there is no superior class of citizen. "There is no caste here," he said.

Our Constitution is color-blind, and neither knows nor tolerates classes among citizens. In respect of civil rights all citizens are equal before the law. The humblest is the peer of the most powerful. The law regards man as man, and takes no account of his surroundings or of his color when his civil rights as guaranteed by the supreme law of the land are involved. It is, therefore, to be regretted that this high tribunal, the final expositer of the fundamental law of the land, has reached the conclusion that it is competent for a State to regulate the enjoyment by citizens of their civil rights solely upon the basis of race. . . . The arbitrary separation of citizens, on the basis of race, while they are on a public highway, is a badge of servitude wholly inconsistent with the civil freedom and the equality before the law established by the Constitution. It cannot be justified upon any legal ground.

Harlan prophesied accurately that the majority opinion would stimulate brutal and irritating aggressions on the rights of Negroes and defeat the purposes of the Civil War Amendments. He argued that the

destinies of the two races, in this country, are indissolubly linked to-gether, and the interests of both require that the common government of all shall not permit the seeds of race hate to be planted under the sanction of law. What can more certainly arouse race hate, what more certainly create and perpetuate a feeling of distrust between these races, than state enactments, which, in fact, proceed on the ground that colored citizens are so inferior and degraded that they cannot be allowed to sit in public coaches occupied by white citizens? That, as all will admit, is the real meaning of such legislation as was enacted in Louisiana. . . . The thin disguise of "equal" accomodations for passengers in railroad coaches will not mislead any one, nor atone for the wrong this day done.

Today, with the advantage of nearly seventy years of hindsight, it is clear that Harlan's opinion is in the great tradition of Ameri-

ca's finest democratic ideals. One authority observed that the
majority opinion was a "compound of bad logic, bad history, bad
sociology, and bad Constitutional law. It ignored and ran counter to the history of the Civil Rights Act of 1886, the Freedmen's
Bureau Act, the Fourteenth Amendment, and subsequent sup-
plementary legislation, the firm purpose of all of which was to
uproot unequal laws, customs, and traditions. It accepted un-
critically either expressly or implicitly the vogue in social thinking in 1896 as reflected by theories of racial supremacy and social
Darwinism. More important, it ran counter to the Court's earlier
decisions. . . ."[1] In contrast, Harlan's dissent "was characterized
by sound logic, accurate history as far as it went, correct constitutional law, and, above all these, high moral assumptions and
aspirations." [2]

Nevertheless, the Court had now given its approval to the
dominant mores of the American community. With few exceptions, newspapers, both North and South, endorsed the Court's
opinion. The *Atlanta Journal* announced proudly that Georgia
"was the first of the Southern States to adopt the policy of providing the same class of railroad accomodations for whites and
Negroes, keeping them separate, of course. This is just. When
Negroes pay the same fare as whites they should receive as good
accommodations. Separate cars for the races are advantageous to
both. They prevent frequent disturbances and the Negroes generally prefer this arrangement." The *New York Journal* observed
that the Louisiana law was a "simple police regulation which any
state has a perfect right to sanction."

With uncanny accuracy Harlan prophesied in his dissent that
the Court's holding would, in time, "prove to be quite as per-
nicious as the decision made by this tribunal in the Dred Scott
case." In the years following the Plessy ruling that separate but
equal facilities were constitutional, racial segregation became

[1] Robert J. Harris, *The Quest for Equality* (Baton Rouge: Louisiana State
University Press, 1960), p. 101.
[2] *Ibid.*, p. 102.

deeply entrenched as a way of life. Segregated, largely deprived
of the right to vote, subject always to terror and violence, the
Negro was kept in a state of complete inferiority. In case after
case the separate but equal doctrine was followed but not re-
examined. Actually, the equal part of the doctrine had no real
meaning, for the Supreme Court refused to look beyond lower
court holdings to find if the segregated facilities for Negroes
were in fact equal to these provided for whites. As a result many
Negro accommodations were said to be equal when everyone knew
that they were decidedly inferior. President Truman's Committee
on Civil Rights remarked aptly in 1947 that the separate but
equal doctrine "is one of the outstanding myths of American
history for it is almost always true that while indeed separate,
these facilities are far from equal. Throughout the segregated
public institutions, Negroes have been denied an equal share of
tax supported services and facilities." [1]

Segregation and numerous other devices made the drive for
Negro equality a slow and painful one indeed. At first, it was
only a handful of dedicated clergymen who fought in behalf of
"an outraged, heartbroken, bruised and bleeding, but God-fear-
ing people." Later groups, such as the National Association for
the Advancement of Colored People, which was founded in 1910,
began to win important victories in the drive for Negro equality.
Race relations committees were formed. Church leaders and
educators began to speak out against segregation. Novelists wrote
of the evils of segregation. Beginning in 1938 the Supreme Court
became much more strict about the equality requirements of
Negro facilities. In subsequent cases the Court continued to in-
sist upon equal accommodations for Negroes. But by 1950 the
Court had made it clear that the "separate but equal" principle
could not be applied in practice in the field of higher education.

By mid-century the Plessy rule was under severe attack. The
walls of segregation were beginning to crumble. American Ne-

[1] *To Secure These Rights* (Washington, D. C.: Government Printing
Office, 1947), pp. 81-82.

groes had not only won many battles in the courts, but their status had been improved considerably by a variety of other factors. The defeat of Nazi Germany and its cult of racial superiority in 1945 had deprived the doctrine of Negro inferiority of its intellectual justification. Moreover, as the horrible Nazi crimes against the Jewish people were unmasked, Americans became increasingly aware of the terrible dangers inherent in theories of racial supremacy. Negroes acquired greater political rights in many urban centers of the North, such as Philadelphia and New York, where they held the balance of power in close elections. At the same time, increasing numbers of Negroes were voting in southern states. World War II and the period of prosperity that followed created new demands for manpower and brought increased employment opportunities for Negroes. The industrialization and unionization of the South after the war also created new job opportunities. The armed forces eliminated segregation. A number of states ended segregation in the national guard. Theaters were desegregated. Negro baseball players joined the major leagues. Time and the course of events seemed to be vindicating Harlan's lonely stand.

Justice Harlan Concurring

It fell to Chief Justice Earl Warren to undo the great evil against which Justice Harlan had protested in vain. To future generations of Americans, Warren will undoubtedly be best known as the author of the historic decision of *Brown* v. *Board of Education*, which held that segregation in public schools is unconstitutional.

Unlike Harlan, Chief Justice Warren grew up in a relatively poor family. Born in Los Angeles, Warren's father was a hardworking railroad mechanic of Norwegian stock. His mother was the daughter of Swedish immigrants. Eager for an education, Warren worked his way through the University of California

and took his law degree at its law school in 1912. He was admitted to the bar in 1914, and practiced law for a brief period
before embarking upon a successful political career. Starting at
the bottom of the California political ladder, he first served as
an assistant city and county attorney. In 1925 he became district
attorney of Alameda County (Oakland), where he made an
enviable record as an honest and vigorous prosecutor of grafters
and other lawbreakers. In 1938 he was elected state Attorney
General, and four years later he became Governor of California.
Warren won the governorship as a Republican, but he was re-
elected twice with the support of Democrats as well as Republicans. He was the only man ever elected to three successive terms
as California's Governor. By 1948 the popularity of his liberal
administration had made him a national figure and he became
Republican candidate for Vice President. Former President Harry
S. Truman, who often praised Warren, once remarked, "Warren
is really a Democrat, but doesn't know it."

Although his political record was impressive, Warren had no
prior judicial experience when President Eisenhower named him
chief justice in 1953—the first chief justice ever appointed from
west of the Mississippi. As the new leader of the Court he quickly
restored a sense of unity and "has already displayed greater
eminence as an administrator than any court head since Hughes."
Moreover, it quickly became apparent that under Warren the
Court was to become increasingly concerned with the protection
of individual liberties, and especially the rights of Negroes.

Speaking for a unanimous Court, Warren's short, lucid opinion
in *Brown* v. *Board of Education* minced no words. The meaning
was crystal clear. He noted that in approaching the problem
of segregation in the public schools the Court "cannot turn the
clock back to 1868 when the Amendment [fourteenth] was
adopted, or even to 1896 when *Plessy* v. *Ferguson* was written.
We must consider public education in the light of its full development and its present place in American life throughout the
Nation. Only in this way can it be determined if segregation in

public schools deprives these plaintiffs of the equal protection of the laws." Quoting excerpts from a lower court case, Warren stated, "Segregation of white and colored children in public schools has a detrimental effect upon the colored children. The impact is greater when it has the sanction of law; for the policy of separating the races is usually interpreted as denoting the inferiority of the Negro group. A sense of inferiority affects the motivation of a child to learn. Segregation with the sanction of law, therefore, has a tendency to retard the educational and mental development of Negro children and to deprive them of some of the benefits they would receive in a racially integrated school." Finally, Warren argued that "any language in *Plessy* v. *Ferguson* contrary to this finding is rejected. We conclude that in the field of public education the doctrine of 'separate but equal' has no place. Separate educational facilities are inherently unequal."

Shortly after the Brown decision, a *New York Times* editorial entitled "Justice Harlan Concurring" paid this tribute to the fiery Kentuckian.

It is eighty-six years since the Fourteenth Amendment was proclaimed a part of the United States Constitution. It is fifty-eight years since the Supreme Court, with Justice Harlan dissenting, established the doctrine of 'separate but equal' provision for the white and Negro races on interstate carriers. It is forty-three years since John Marshall Harlan passed from this earth. Now the words he used in his lonely dissent . . . in the case of *Plessy* v. *Ferguson* in 1896 have become in effect by last Monday's unanimous decision of the Supreme Court a part of the law of the land. . . .

Last Monday's case dealt solely with segregation in the schools, but there was not one word in Chief Justice Warren's opinion that was inconsistent with the earlier views of Justice Harlan. This is an instance in which the voice crying in the wilderness finally becomes the expression of a people's will and in which justice overtakes and thrusts aside a timorous expediency.[1]

[1] *The New York Times*, May 23, 1954, Sec. 4, p. 10E. Copyright by *The New York Times*. Reprinted by permission.

Today, little, if anything, of *Plessy* v. *Ferguson* remains. In addition to the public schools, the courts have held to be unconstitutional all segregation in public parks, municipal housing projects, public golf courses, public beaches and buses. And despite the tragedy of Little Rock and the University of Mississippi, the direction of events is unmistakable. This would have pleased Justice Harlan. "Perhaps the most satisfying aspect to Harlan in the present situation would be the part played by the Supreme Court of the United States. Harlan maintained an unswerving faith in the role of the Supreme Court as defender of the citizen's liberties and guardian of American constitutional ideals. That the Supreme Court . . . has become the guiding force of the new reconstruction, in the spirit of his dissents on the segregation issue, may be seen as a particularly fitting vindication of John Marshall Harlan's faith."[1]

The lone voice crying in the wilderness has swelled to a mighty chorus that will not be stilled until the great wrong of segregation has been forever abolished from our shores. Perhaps somewhere old Justice Harlan—little respected by doughty Justice Holmes who referred to him as "the last of the tobacco-spitting justices" and dismissed by Justice Frankfurter as an "eccentric exception"—looks down upon us and says to himself: "If only they had listened—how much easier it would have been!"

[1] Alan F. Westin, *Yale Law Journal, op. cit.,* p. 710.

IV

Justice Oliver W. Holmes
and *United States* v. *Schwimmer*

*Of how a solid Back Bay Republican aristocrat, thrice
wounded in the Civil War, fought on behalf of a pacifist
whose ideas he abhorred.*

THE MAN

OLIVER WENDELL HOLMES, JR. is undoubtedly the best-known
Supreme Court Justice in American history. The story of his life
has been dramatized on stage and television. Scholars continue
to probe into every conceivable aspect of Holmes' life and philosophy. Hundreds of articles about him have been written. He
was the subject of a fictionalized popular biography—*Yankee
from Olympus*—which was widely read. More often than not
Holmes is classified with the giants of American history: Washington, Jefferson, and Lincoln. No other justice, with the exception of John Marshall, has been so widely acclaimed.

Seldom in our history has a Supreme Court justice so captured
the imagination of the American people. Holmes did so largely
because he could be "in a praiseworthy sense, all things to all
people. To the iconoclast, he is the great dissenter; to the liberal,

he is the hero of the rebellion against judicial arrogance; to the conservative, a New England Yankee skeptical of economic nostrums; to the soldier, an apostle of war; to the philosopher, a gifted amateur honoring ideas above worldly accomplishment; to the jurist, an inexhaustible source of history and legal purposes." [1] Writing in 1941, a noted scholar remarked, "It has taken a decade to elevate Mr. Justice Holmes from Deity to Mortality."

To even attempt to capture Holmes in a few brief pages is an act of presumption. There is too much to tell. There are too many strands. The attempt here will be to simply bring out the high points of his life and work.

From beginning to end Holmes was an aristocrat—born on the right side of the tracks in Boston on March 8, 1841. His father, a distinguished physician and poet, was at the center of the literary and intellectual life of New England. His mother, Amelia Lee Jackson, was the daughter of an associate justice of the Massachusetts Supreme Court and descendant of a long line of leading merchants and bankers.

Holmes' youthful activities were centered around school. He attended Boston Latin School and later the private classes of Mr. Epes S. Dixwell, whose eldest daughter Holmes later married. From an early age Holmes was unable to please his well-known father, "the autocrat at the breakfast table," who criticized his physical shortcomings and his lack of literary taste. But Holmes' difficulties with his father played an important part in his later life. Holmes' official biographer has pointed out that "the mind and temperament of Dr. Holmes had both stimulated and irritated his son, leading him to make his father's larger qualities a standard to be followed and his smaller failings an example to be rejected." [2] Holmes once said that his father had

[1] Walker Lowry, "Mr. Justice Holmes: The Community vs. the Individual," *California Law Review*, XXXVI (September, 1948), 390.

[2] Mark De Wolfe Howe, *Justice Oliver Wendell Holmes: The Shaping Years, 1841-1870* (Cambridge: Harvard University Press, 1957), p. 285.

a "fertile and suggestive intellect. I do not care as much as he would have liked me to for his novels and poetry—but I think he had the most penetrating mind of all that [Boston] lot." [1]

Since "his family had been in the habit of securing a college education," it was only natural that Holmes, like his grand-fathers, father, uncles, and cousins, should go to Harvard. He entered Harvard at sixteen and was graduated four years later in July, 1861, shortly after the outbreak of the Civil War. A few days later he was commissioned a First Lieutenant in the Twenti-eth Regiment, Massachusetts Volunteers. In September Holmes started South with his unit to join the Army of the Potomac and to witness some of the bloodiest fighting of the war. He was wounded three times. At Ball's Bluff he was shot in the chest and narrowly escaped death; at Antietam he was shot in the neck and thought by some to have been killed; at Chancellorsville a piece of shrapnel shattered a heel and caused an injury that was to trouble him for years to come. For Holmes the war was now over. He was tired, exhausted, and filled with despair. In 1864 he was discharged with the rank of Captain.

The Civil War had a deep effect on Holmes. He never quite forgot the terrible suffering, the dysentery, the flies, the broken and dead young bodies. The tragedy of it all matured him; it helped make him a skeptic; above all, it made him keenly aware of the fragility of human existence. Over the years one could catch glimpses of what he had learned during the war. Once he said, "Perhaps as long as man dwells upon the globe, his destiny is battle, and he has to take the chances of war." [2] With a group of Civil War veterans he shared these thoughts:

Through our great good fortune in our youth our hearts were touched with fire. It was given us to learn at the outset that life is a profound and passionate thing. While we are permitted to scorn nothing but

[1] *Ibid.*, p. 19.
[2] The quotations from Holmes' speeches used in these pages are from his book: *Speeches* (Boston: Little, Brown, 1934), and are reprinted by per-mission.

indifference, and do not pretend to undervalue the worldly rewards of ambition, we have seen with our own eyes, beyond and above the gold fields, the snowy heights of honor, and it is for us to bear the report to those who come after us. But, above all, we have learned that whether a man accepts from Fortune her spade and will look downward and dig, or from Aspiration her axe and cord and will scale the ice, the one and only success which it is his to command is to bring to his work a mighty heart.

Holmes described war as "horrible and dull. It is only when time has passed that you see that its message was divine. I hope it may be long before we are called again to sit at the master's feet. But some teacher of the kind we all need. In this snug, over-safe corner of the world we need it, that we may realize that our comfortable routine is no eternal necessity of things, but merely a little space of calm in the midst of the tempestuous untamed streaming of the world, and in order that we may be ready for danger."

The attractive young war hero returned home to the plaudits of the crowd—particularly the young ladies of Boston. But Holmes paid little attention to them. He was trying to decide what to do with his life! In the fall of 1864 he entered the Harvard Law School. He was still confused—not sure that he really wanted to study law. He had considered other careers—writing, art, philosophy, and even medicine, but in the end he gave himself completely to the law. In 1866 he graduated from the law school and was admitted to the bar the following year. Holmes began to practice law in Boston. Deeply ambitious, he worked hard to gain recognition.

Holmes rose rapidly, largely because he applied himself with feverish intensity to every task at hand. However, in June 1872, Holmes did take enough time away from his duties as a practicing lawyer, lecturer at Harvard, and editor of the *American Law Review* to marry Fanny Bowditch Dixwell whom he had known for many years. The new Mrs. Holmes was a charming, witty woman with "a genius for affection" whose family "represented

the complex traditions of Cambridge; cultivated, less than afflu-
ent, yet dignified by the blood of New England's worthies, they
occupied a position between the fashionable world of Boston,
the learned community of Harvard, and the clerical world of
New England." [1] From the time of her marriage Fanny Dixwell
became completely dedicated "to the happiness, success and
tranquility of her husband." For fifty-six years, until her death in
1929, she helped to mold his career and work.

In 1873 Holmes edited the twelfth edition of James Kent's
four-volume work, *Commentaries on American Law,* which was
then the standard work for American lawyers. The three years
spent on this work gave Holmes an unmatched familiarity with
American law, and helped him become one of the most able and
best informed lawyers of his time. But his greatest scholarly contribution was yet to come. In 1881 he published *The Common
Law,* which gradually won recognition as a landmark in the realistic study of American law. For a year Holmes had denied himself every pleasure, including sleep, in order to complete the book.
It was well worth the effort, for its publication marked a turning
point in his career. The book won wide acclaim. Holmes' reputation was made. In 1882 he was offered a professorship at Harvard, but after teaching only one term, he accepted an appointment to the Massachusetts Supreme Court—a position he had
long wanted.

Holmes served on the highest state court with distinction for
twenty years, the last three as chief justice. During that period
he made significant contributions in many areas of law through
nearly 1,300 opinions. He was already sixty-one years old when
President Theodore Roosevelt named him to the Supreme Court
to fill the vacancy created by the resignation of Justice Horace
Gray, an outstanding legal historian who also hailed from Boston.
Holmes carved out an entirely new career for himself on the
Supreme Court. He was destined to serve there for thirty years

[1] Mark De Wolfe Howe, *op. cit.,* p. 199.

and to make perhaps the most significant contributions to American Constitutional law since John Marshall's time.

Holmes' pragmatic conception of law, which emerged from his years on the Court, was first expressed in the opening sentences of *The Common Law*, written before he was forty. There he said:

The life of the law has not been logic: it has been experience. The felt necessities of the time, the prevalent moral and political theories, intuitions of public policy, avowed or unconscious, even the prejudices which judges share with their fellow-men, have had a good deal more . to do than syllogism in determining the rules by which men should be governed. The law embodies the story of a nation's development through many centuries, and it cannot be dealt with as if it contained only the axioms and corollaries of a book of mathematics. In order to know what it is, we must know what it has been, and what it tends to become. We must alternately consult history and existing theories of legislation.

This view of the nature of law logically led Holmes to condemn judicial interference with legislative bodies. He himself had little faith in reform. A true product of the age of Darwin with its belief in the competitive struggle for existence resulting in the survival of the fittest, Holmes was skeptical about legislative programs to better the lot of mankind. Speaking in New York in 1913 he said, "I have no belief in panaceas and almost none in sudden ruin." He thought that American socialists and reformers in general were fools and the "greatest bores in the world." Yet even when he disagreed, he saw no reason why courts should block programs that the people seemed to want. He saw clearly that he had no right to read his own private notions into the Constitution. Thus he dissented courageously and eloquently when the Court declared unconstitutional the liberal laws on wages, hours, child labor, etc., that were being demanded by the rising industrial class. But in the area of civil liberties Holmes was not willing to grant as much leeway to legislative bodies, particularly when freedom of speech or procedural fairness in criminal prosecutions was involved.

It was natural that the general public should come to know Holmes as a great liberal dissenter. Yet Holmes was a political conservative little concerned for the welfare of the great mass of men. Unlike his friend, Justice Brandeis, Holmes was not a zealous reformer. Although he and Brandeis often found themselves in agreement, they arrived at the same conclusions by widely different paths. Brandeis was the scientist using statistics, economics and any other available tool of the social scientist to support his conclusions. He was a passionate crusader who could not stand aloof from the conflicts of his day. He condemned slums, sweatshops and injustices of any kind wherever they were found. Holmes, on the other hand, was the detached, skeptical, Olympian philosopher of the law who "showed no dominant inclination to shape economic forces constructively. His contributions to our liberalism are essentially negative. Holmes is the enlightened skeptic; Brandeis, the militant Crusader." [1] In short, "A Brandeis sustains a new industrial or business regulation because he sees and demonstrates its utility. A Holmes sustains it in mild wondering approval, patient tolerance, magnificent disinterest." [2]

How was it possible for Holmes—a solid Back Bay Republican aristocrat strongly committed to the prejudices of his class—to emerge as a liberal, albeit a negative, spokesman for liberal democracy? The answer is to be found in the fact that Holmes was a New England intellectual. As such he attached great importance to ideas. In fact, he had a genuine respect for intellectual endeavor. He had read the writings of all the great thinkers. Throughout his life he was on intimate terms with the intellectual elite of both England and America. He knew the importance of allowing each man to have his say—to express his ideas regardless of how foolish they might appear to others. For Holmes, freedom of the mind was the most crucial of all public values.

But at the same time Holmes had a cosmic view, which made him skeptical and humble before the mysteries of the universe. In the long view of history, perhaps nothing mattered very much. Thus he wondered openly "if cosmically an idea is any more important than the bowels" or if man has any more significance than a baboon or a grain of sand. This view of the world made it impossible for Holmes to subscribe to any legal or philosophical absolutes. He did not share the New Englander's belief in God. For him the Christian's explanation of life was too simple, too pat. Yet he possessed a mystic faith in a power larger than himself, which he could not understand. "I think it not improbable," he once said in a New York speech, "that man, like the grub that prepares a chamber for the winged thing it never has seen but is to be—that man may have cosmic destinies that he does not understand. And so beyond the vision of battling races and an impoverished earth I catch a dreaming glimpse of peace."

Holmes was not a humanitarian. Neither was he, on many occasions, a kindly or understanding person. He could not suffer fools gladly. But even though at times it was hard to perceive, Holmes had learned the "Great lesson of life"—humility.

It is this humility, this refusal to read his own experiences and beliefs into the Constitution, and his alertness in opposing judicial associates who, often unconsciously, did so, that constitutes the genius of Holmes. He did not confuse his personal tastes and distastes with constitutional necessity. And so when his associates read a pseudo-laissez-faire into the law of the land, and show marked hostility to offensive speech, Holmes was apt to be in dissent. But he was outspokenly skeptical of the reforms involved in most of the great opinions which he wrote in support of legislative freedom to adopt them; as in the famous free speech dissents he openly disdained the ideas whose utterance he defended. Thus on a bedrock of humility and skepticism Holmes laid the foundation for an abiding democratic philosophy.[1]

Perhaps nothing better demonstrates Holmes' commitment to the liberal democratic creed than his devastating dissenting opinion in *United States* v. *Schwimmer*, the last of his free speech dissents delivered in the twilight years of his life. In that opinion he revealed clearly his philosophy of toleration and demonstrated, as Justice Cardozo once said, "that law in his hands has been philosophy, but it has been literature too."

THE CASE

Madame Rosika Schwimmer was not an ordinary woman. As a result, many Americans thought of her as an odd, somewhat forbidding person. Born in Hungary in 1877, Mrs. Schwimmer was well-educated and highly intelligent. She prided herself on being an absolute atheist. In 1904 she was the youngest delegate to the International Womens' Suffrage Alliance meeting in Berlin. Within a few years she became an internationally known linguist, lecturer, and writer of childrens' stories and books on public questions. A sensitive, serious woman, Madame Schwimmer was an uncompromising pacifist who worked unflaggingly to bring an end to World War I. It was her devotion to the cause of peace that had inspired Henry Ford to send his "peace ship" to Europe in 1915 to "get the boys out of the trenches by Christmas."

In August, 1921, Mrs. Schwimmer renounced her allegiance to Hungary, left Europe and settled in Illinois because she felt that the United States was "the nation most likely to lead in building a world federation which would end the militarist epoch." In November of the same year she declared her intention to become

[1] Wallace Mendelson, *Capitalism and the Supreme Court* (New York: Appleton-Century-Crofts, 1960), pp. 75-76.

an American citizen. During the next few years Mrs. Schwimmer continued to lecture and write in the cause of peace. Her activities found little favor among self-styled patriotic groups such as the Womens' Auxiliary of the American Legion who urged the Naturalization Bureau to deny her petition for citizenship.

In September, 1926, Mrs. Schwimmer completed the five years residence requirement and filed her final petition for naturalization. She was one of nearly a quarter million candidates for citizenship during the year. After having answered a questionnaire submitted by a naturalization official and corresponding with him concerning her pacifist views, she finally appeared in a Federal District Court in Chicago on November 14, 1927. The presiding judge, George A. Carpenter, noted that in the questionnaire Mrs. Schwimmer was asked, "If necessary, are you willing to take up arms in defense of this country?" Her reply in the questionnaire was, "I would not take up arms personally." Asked to explain, Mrs. Schwimmer stated as follows: "I am able to take the oath of allegiance without any reservations. I am willing to do everything that an American citizen has to do except fighting. If American women would be compelled to do that, I would not do that. I am an uncompromising pacifist. I do not care how many other women fight, because I consider it a question of conscience. I am not willing to bear arms. In every other single way I am ready to follow the law and do everything that the law compels American citizens to do."

Mrs. Schwimmer said that her refusal to take up arms did not contradict the oath of allegiance. There were other ways and means to fulfill her duty to support and defend the Constitution and laws. "All my past work proves," she said, "that I have always served democratic ideals and fought—though not with arms— against undemocratic institutions." She testified that she could not compromise her beliefs by lying in the questionnaire even though, for all practical purposes, she would never be called to take up arms. "I have no sense of nationalism," she said, "only a cosmic consciousness of belonging to the human family, shared by all those who believe that all human beings are the children of God."

Following the testimony before the Court, Judge Carpenter denied Mrs. Schwimmer's application for citizenship, holding that she "is not attached to the principles of the Constitution of the United States and well disposed to the good order and happiness of the same, and further that she is unable to take the oath of allegiance prescribed by the Naturalization Law without a mental reservation." Still anxious to become an American citizen and believing sincerely that her views of citizenship entitled her to naturalization, Mrs. Schwimmer took her case to a Federal Circuit Court of Appeals.

On June 29, 1928, the Circuit Court of Appeals in a unanimous opinion, reversed the district court and ordered that Mrs. Schwimmer's application for naturalization be granted. The Court minced no words. Judge Albert B. Anderson, in delivering the opinion, noted that the case did not involve a male applicant young enough to bear arms but rather a woman of fifty years of age. If she became a citizen, she could not under the law be required to shoulder a gun. Nor was it likely that she would ever be called to war. "In other words," said Judge Anderson, "there is put to her a hypothetical question—what would she do under circumstances that never have occurred and probably never will occur—and upon her answers to this supposed case her petition is denied. A petitioner's rights are not to be determined by putting conundrums to her."

Despite the unanimous decision of the circuit court, the government decided to carry the case to the Supreme Court. On May 27, 1929, the Court reversed the circuit court decision and thereby allowed to stand the original ruling denying Mrs. Schwimmer citizenship. Ironically enough, the Court's decision was handed down just nine months to the day after the United States and other nations had signed the Kellogg-Briand pact which solemnly renounced war as an instrument of national policy and declared that all future disputes were to be settled by peaceful means only.

The Court divided six to three, with Justice Pierce Butler writing the majority opinion. Butler declared that "the duty of citizens by force of arms to defend our government against all enemies whenever necessity arises is a fundamental principle of the Constitution." He reasoned that a person like Mrs. Schwimmer without any sense of nationalism "is not well bound or held by the ties of affection to any nation or government. Such persons are liable to be incapable of the attachment for and devotion to the principles of our Constitution that is required of aliens seeking naturalization." Butler concluded that the burden was upon Mrs. Schwimmer to show "that her pacifism and lack of nationalistic sense did not oppose the principle that it is a duty of citizenship by force of arms when necessary to defend the country against all enemies . . . she failed to do so." Therefore the district court had no choice but to deny her application for citizenship.

Justice Edward T. Sanford dissented, stating simply that he agreed with the decision of the circuit court. Justice Brandeis concurred with Holmes' dissenting opinion.

When Holmes wrote his Schwimmer dissent, he was already eighty-eight years of age—the oldest man who has ever held a seat on the Court. Moreover, he was a very lonely old man for on April 30, 1929, less than a month before the Schwimmer decision was announced, his beloved wife had died. Her death was a severe blow. Holmes felt that half of his life had been snatched away. To Frederick Pollock he wrote that his wife made "life poetry for me and at 88 one must be ready for the end. I shall keep at work and interested while it lasts—though not caring very much for how long." [1] To his admirer, Dr. John C. H. Wu, Holmes wrote that he was substantially finished. "You may have heard before this of the death of my wife, which not only takes

[1] Mark De Wolfe Howe, (ed.) *Holmes–Pollock Letters* (Cambridge: Harvard University Press, 1941), p. 243.

away a half of my life, but gives me notice. She was of the same age as I and at 88 the end is due. I may work on for a year or two, but I cannot hope to add much to what I have done." [1]

But the old soldier carried on as he had done on the battle-fields of the Civil War seventy years before. Wounded three times, he had a personal knowledge of the horror and at times, the necessity of war. He had little sympathy for an extremist, such as he considered Mrs. Schwimmer. On April 13, 1929, after a Court conference, he had written to Harold Laski about the case. "What damned fools people are who believe things," he said. "A case [Schwimmer] has gone over for further considera-tion, of a woman wanting to become a citizen, but who, being as she says, more of a pacifist than Jane Addams, has to explain that she would not fight for the Constitution (or, as her counsel said, wouldn't do what the law wouldn't let her do) and so opens to the Government a discourse on the foundation of the Constitution being in readiness to defend itself by force. All 'isms seem to me silly—but this hyperaethereal respect for human life seems per-haps the silliest of all." [2]

Yet Holmes dissented. "About seventy-five years ago I learned I was not God," Holmes once remarked to his friend and admirer, Justice Harlan F. Stone. In his Schwimmer dissent Holmes gave dramatic proof of this spirit of objectivity and toleration with irony, grace and wit. His words speak for themselves.

The applicant seems to be a woman of superior character and intelli-gence, obviously more than ordinarily desirable as a citizen of the United States. It is agreed that she is qualified for citizenship except so far as the views set forth in a statement of facts. . . . The views referred to are an extreme opinion in favor of pacifism and a state-ment that she would not bear arms to defend the Constitution. So far

[1] *Justice Holmes to Doctor Wu: An Intimate Correspondence, 1921–1932* (New York: Central Book, not dated), p. 53.

[2] Mark De Wolfe Howe, (ed.) *Holmes–Laski Letters* (Cambridge: Har-vard University Press, 1953), p. 1146.

as the adequacy of her oath is concerned I hardly can see how that is affected by the statement, inasmuch as she is a woman over fifty years of age, and would not be allowed to bear arms if she wanted to. And as to the opinion, the whole examination of the applicant shows that she holds none of the now-dreaded creeds, but thoroughly believes in organized government and prefers that of the United States to any other in the world. Surely it cannot show lack of attachment to the principles of the Constitution that she thinks that it can be improved. I suppose that most intelligent people think that it might be. Her particular improvement looking to the abolition of war seems to me not materially different in its bearing on this case from a wish to establish cabinet government as in England, or a single house, or one term of seven years for the President.

Holmes saved the most telling blows for the final paragraph of his opinion. The sentences that follow have been among the most widely quoted in our constitutional law.

She [Mrs. Schwimmer] is an optimist and states in strong and, I do not doubt, sincere words her belief that war will disappear and that the impending destiny of mankind is to unite in peaceful leagues. I do not share that optimism nor do I think that a philosophical view of the world would regard war as absurd. But most people who have known it regard it with horror, as a last resort, and even if not yet ready for cosmopolitan efforts, would welcome any practicable combinations that would increase the power on the side of peace. The notion that the applicant's optimistic anticipation would make her a worse citizen is sufficiently answered by her examination, which seems to me a better argument for her admission than any that I can offer. Some of her answers might excite popular prejudice, but if there is any principle of the Constitution that more imperatively calls for attachment than any other it is the principle of free thought—not free thought for those who agree with us but freedom for the thought that we hate. I think that we should adhere to that principle with regard to admission into, as well as to life within, this country. And recurring to the opinion that bars this applicant's way, I would suggest that the Quakers have done their share to make the country what it is, that

many citizens agree with the applicant's belief, and that I had not
supposed hitherto that we regretted our inability to expel them because they believe more than some of us do in the teachings of the
Sermon on the Mount.

In the Schwimmer opinion Holmes echoed the noble words
written ten years before in his dissent in *Abrams* v. *United States*.
In that most passionate and eloquent defense of freedom of expression Holmes said:

When men have realized that time has upset many fighting faiths,
they may come to believe even more than they believe the very
foundations of their own conduct that the ultimate good desired is
better reached by free trade in ideas—that the best test of truth is
the power of the thought to get itself accepted in the competition of
the market, and that truth is the only ground upon which their wishes
safely can be carried out. That at any rate is the theory of our
Constitution. It is an experiment, as all life is an experiment. Every
year if not every day we have to wager our salvation upon some
prophecy based upon imperfect knowledge. While that experiment is
part of our system I think we should be eternally vigilant against
attempts to check the expression of opinions that we loathe and believe to be fraught with death, unless they so imminently threaten
immediate interference with the lawful and pressing purposes of the
law that an immediate check is required to save the country.

The Schwimmer case caused quite a stir. The Naturalization
Bureau began with increased zeal to expose pacifists seeking
citizenship. The professional patriotic groups, such as the Daughters of the American Revolution, praised the Court's majority
opinion. On May 30, 1929, Elmer Davis, a news commentator
and writer, wrote to *The New York Times*, saying that the decision made it clear "that no one is worthy of American citizenship
except members of the DAR and the Anti-Saloon League. Congress should take up the matter and restrict the franchise by
appropriate legislation!" The *Washington Evening Star* remarked
that Madame Schwimmer "sought to break into the American
family on her own terms. Excepting our professional peace-at-
any-price groups, the republic will applaud the Supreme Court's

finding." A *New York Times* editorial seemed to pay tribute to Holmes but took a peculiarly ambivalent stance. "It is a little anomalous," said the *Times,* "that a country which has renounced war should exclude from its citizenship a person whose chief offense is her opposition to war. *But these are irrelevant reflections. The law is the law."*

Most opposition to the majority opinion came from the churches, religious organizations, peace groups, and the American Civil Liberties Union. The feelings of the opposition were perhaps best summed up by a minister—named, ironically enough, John Haynes Holmes—in a sermon in New York on June 2, 1929.

The case of Madame Schwimmer as decided by the Supreme Court is a perfect illustration of the Christianity that Christians forget. If Christianity is the religion of Jesus, it is the religion of the Sermon on the Mount, and right at the heart of the Sermon on the Mount, as Mr. Justice Holmes pointed out in his minority opinion, is the doctrine of non-violence. I know nothing so characteristic of Jesus as his teaching that men should not use force or take up arms under any conditions and for any purpose. Every true Christian has seen in the idea of non-resistance Jesus' greatest contribution to religious thought. All the early Christians refused to take up arms at the call of the Roman Empire, just as Mrs. Schwimmer has stated that she would refuse to take up arms at the call of the American Republic. We have never dared to rely on anything but the power of superior violence in the hands of the State. If anybody remembers the religion of Jesus in this regard and takes it seriously, we kill them or imprison them as we did the conscientious objectors in time of war or we deny them citizenship as we do Madame Schwimmer in time of peace.

But despite all such efforts, Holmes' views were not to prevail for some time—not until 1946. The story of how his Schwimmer dissent finally became permanently imbedded in American law will be told in the next chapter.

Holmes was now a very old man. Quoting a Latin poet on the evening of his ninetieth birthday, he told a nationwide radio

audience, "Death plucks my ear and says, 'Live, I am coming.'"
But he was still to have another five years. Shortly before his
ninety-first birthday he resigned from the Court. From Washington he wrote to Pollock: "It is wonderful and incredible to have
no duties. I can't tell you how I like it; I ought to be getting
cultivated, for my secretary calculates that, roughly, we have
read 4,500,000 words since we got here, but I am afraid that a
good deal buzzes through my head without much profit to me." [1]

To the end, Holmes loved life. On March 6, 1935, he died of
bronchial pneumonia after a week's illness. Two days later—on
his ninety-fourth birthday—the old soldier was buried beside his
wife in Arlington National Cemetery.

[1] *Holmes–Pollock Letters op. cit.*, p. 309.

V

Chief Justice Charles Evans Hughes
and *United States* v. *Macintosh*

*Of how a stern, dignified Chief Justice, whom many regarded
as a tool of the corporations with no regard for human rights,
argued on behalf of a Baptist minister seeking American
citizenship.*

THE MAN

IT HAS BEEN WELL SAID that Charles Evans Hughes "was the
kind of man that the American people require once every generation if they are to avoid the fate that Ben Franklin feared—
sinking into a despotism from an excess of democracy."[1] Yet,
ironically enough, the American people never really came to
know Hughes during his lifetime. They saw only the exterior
man. The inner warmth and tolerance of Hughes never became
manifest. The public did not picture Hughes as the devoted
father and husband, genial companion and compassionate human
being that he was. Instead, the familiar caricature of Hughes
was that of a cold, austere, humorless automaton—a human icicle
with little concern or feeling for his fellowmen.

This caricature of Hughes prevailed largely because he had

[1] Herbert Elliston, "The Integrity of Justice Hughes," *The Atlantic*, April,
1952 p. 75.

77

few of the qualities needed to endear him to the great masses of men. He never became a "popular" figure in the image of a Franklin D. Roosevelt or a William Jennings Bryan. He was a shy, reserved, self-contained man with little taste for the outward, superficial amiability that has been the trademark of so many successful politicians. He was an intense man, an extremely hard worker with little time for gossip and trivialities. Like Holmes, he did not suffer fools gladly. He had a "positive genius for privacy," and was irritated by unnecessary intrusions. Moreover, the bearded Hughes with his piercing gray eyes was a truly magnificent but unapproachable figure of a man. He looked too Olympian. Even when the flaming red beard had completely faded, Hughes looked much like a "Victorian child's image of Almighty God" who was not to be lightly accosted. Anyone who has gazed upon the magnificent bust of Hughes in the ornate Supreme Court building easily senses the man's Olympian detachment. He gives the appearance of a determined man with a purpose—a man who knows where he is going and what he is about. But, at the same time, there is little of the warmth one sees, for example, in the bust of Chief Justice Stone directly across from that of Hughes. As a journalist once so aptly put it, Hughes looked like a "Viking in a frock-coat."

Yet Hughes won the respect and admiration of his generation, largely because it could perceive his statesmanlike qualities. Certainly few men in American history "have packed so much and such superlative accomplishment into a single lifetime." Throughout his adult life Hughes was a leading corporation lawyer and a respected pillar of the bar. During a brief interlude of teaching at Cornell University he won the admiration of his academic colleagues. He was a strong reform Governor of New York, capable Associate Justice of the Supreme Court, presidential candidate who barely missed the White House, an outstanding Secretary of State, a judge of the Permanent Court of International Justice, and finally, a most powerful and respected Chief Justice in a revolutionary period of American life.

Hughes was born in Glens Falls, New York, on April 11, 1862. His father was a deeply devoted Baptist minister who had come to America from Wales in 1855. His mother, who had grown up in one of the closely-knit Dutch communities of New York state, had been a school teacher, extremely well educated, with a remarkable proficiency in mathematics. Hughes—the only child— once said that his parents were "brought together in a spiritual union which held them in the closest companionship as they pursued the same aims and cherished the same hopes. . . . Their love for each other, which at the outset had surmounted the obstacles raised by the differences in their early environment and in temperament, grew in strength throughout the forty-nine years of their union, as they labored together in unity of spirit for a common cause and with a profound faith. I have never known any persons more sincere in what they professed or more constantly dominated by a sense of religious duty." [1]

From the beginning Hughes was a serious minded youngster. At home he was given intensive training in religious matters. At the same time the needs of his lively mind were not neglected. His mother taught him to read at the age of three and a half. By the time he was five Hughes had memorized many of the family prayers. At six he found school too easy and boring. After a few weeks, he resumed his studies at home. His mother taught him German and mathematics. His father gave him intensive lessons in Greek. Both parents guided Hughes' reading into constructive channels and instilled in him their own great love of books.

At ten, when Hughes was ready to enter school again, his father acquired another church in Newark, New Jersey. Shortly thereafter the family moved to New York City where the Reverend Mr. Hughes continued to crusade against all sorts of "evils," including tobacco and liquor. Young Hughes thus went to public schools in both Newark and New York and was graduated when he was only thirteen. At fourteen, he entered Madison

[1] Merlo J. Pusey, *Charles Evans Hughes* (New York: Macmillan, 1951), I, 4. Reprinted by permission.

College (now Colgate University) to prepare for the Baptist ministry. Hughes found college life an exhilarating experience indeed. He was glad to be away from home. "The strict regimen to which he had been subjected since his infancy had created in him a distaste for religious formalities and a longing for freedom to follow his own inclinations. As a minister's son, he had been expected to be a little angel—to attend all the church gatherings, to be an example to the other boys, to neglect nothing. Anything resembling sports or even pleasure on Sunday was tabooed. While his mind was receptive to religious teachings, his parents overgorged him, with the effect of defeating the very purpose to which they were so conscientiously devoting themselves." [1]

It took Hughes only two years to become dissatisfied with the then rural, provincial atmosphere of Colgate. He longed for a more liberal, less restricted environment. This he found at Brown University, where he completed his college education at the age of nineteen with high honors. At Brown, much to the disappointment of his parents and especially his mother, Hughes decided to give up the ministry for a career in law. But since he had no money, he took a position teaching Greek, Latin, and Mathematics at a private school in Delhi, New York, for a salary of $200 per year. He left after one school year to enter Columbia Law School on a scholarship. At Columbia he supported himself by tutoring and by part-time work in a prominent New York law firm. He was graduated at the top of his class in 1884 and was awarded a coveted three-year fellowship which paid him $500 per year in return for night tutoring at the law school. At the same time he became a full-time law clerk in the firm he had served as a student.

Hughes was now well on his way. Within a few years he became a partner in the revamped firm of Carter, Hughes and Cravath which later became extremely prosperous. On December 5, 1888, he married Antoinette Carter, a graduate of Wellesley College and daughter of the firm's senior partner. His marriage

[1] *Ibid.*, p. 25.

was indeed the "happiest venture of his life." Like Holmes, Hughes was blessed with an intelligent, understanding and loving wife who was constantly by his side during the fifty-seven years of a nearly perfect companionship. When she died on the day after their fifty-seventh wedding anniversary, there was little but loneliness left for the retired Chief Justice.

In the early years after his marriage Hughes actually had little time for home life because of the demands of his practice. He buried himself in his work, driving himself night and day until, in 1891, his health broke down. He left New York for a "happy interlude" of two years as a law professor at Cornell, but returned to plunge again into a lucrative practice with increased vigor. He continued to work at a dizzy pace. This zeal to excel in good work continued throughout his life. He believed deeply in the remark he once made that "life is only work, and then more work, and then more work."

Hughes was catapulted into public fame quite by accident. Deeply immersed in his law practice, he had little time or energy for politics. But in 1905 he was named counsel to a New York State Commission investigating exorbitant rates charged for gas and electricity. His careful investigation forced rates down and brought him a great deal of deserved publicity. Later that year he was named counsel to another state committee investigating insurance companies. In a series of public hearings he brilliantly exposed insurance malpractices and laid the basis for important reform legislation. Hughes' reputation as a crusading investigator won him the Republican nomination for Governor in 1906. He defeated William Randolph Hearst for the office by a close margin—the only Republican candidate for state office to be elected that year. He tackled his new job in Albany with his usual vigor and zeal. He fired scores of political hacks and filled important state jobs with honest men of real ability. He ran the state government efficiently and refused to compromise with party leaders who learned, too late, that Hughes really meant what he said in his campaign speeches. Despite the opposition of the political bosses, Hughes was re-elected in 1908 and served two more years until named to the Supreme Court by President Taft.

Hughes served on the Court until 1916 when he resigned to accept the Republican nomination for the Presidency. He had not asked for the nomination. He was very uneasy about a Supreme Court justice leaving the bench for rough-and-tumble politics. In fact, he regretted leaving the Court. Yet when the nomination came he felt that he had no alternative but to accept it as a call to higher duty.

Hughes' presidential campaign marked the low point of his brilliant public career. The Republicans made many mistakes. Hughes himself conducted a poor campaign. His speeches lacked fire and conviction. He tried too hard to please too many diverse elements in both parties. He played it safe, and thereby was unable to offer a program which might lift men's hearts. Yet the election was astonishingly close. On election night Hughes went to bed believing that he would be elected. A number of newspapers had already declared him the winner! But, as the votes came in, it became clear within the next few days that Wilson had won by carrying California by the slender margin of 3,775 votes. The final electoral vote was 277 for President Wilson and 254 for Hughes.

Hughes accepted the defeat without rancor or bitterness and with characteristic grace. Instead of worrying about what might have been, he plunged with renewed vigor into the practice of law. When war broke out, he accepted the chairmanship of the Draft Appeal Board for New York City and later, at the request of President Wilson, launched an investigation of alleged frauds in the aircraft industry that had slowed down the production of military planes. At the end of the war he was back again in a busy and lucrative law practice in New York.

In 1920, when Hughes was undoubtedly the most prominent lawyer in the country, he gave the most courageous demonstration of his passion for justice. The years after World War I were

characterized by a hysterical fear of Bolshevism, which resulted
in a wave of intolerance against every conceivable form of radicalism. In New York State the peak of bigotry was reached when
the state assembly refused to seat five regularly elected Socialist
members from New York City because of their unpopular views.
Within forty-eight hours Hughes voluntarily went to the defense
of the five Socialists protesting that the assembly's action was an
outrageous invasion of the people's right to choose their own
representatives. Though Hughes personally abhorred the principles of the Socialist Party, he went to Albany to testify in behalf
of the five ousted members. But the assembly refused to listen
to his testimony. Hughes then filed a powerful brief concluding,
"If a majority can exclude the whole or a part of the minority
because it deems the political views entertained by them hurtful,
then free government is at an end." But the state legislature was
too caught up in the hysteria of the moment to listen to reason.
It proceeded to expel the Socialists and even outlaw the party.
Nevertheless, Hughes' action "made the conservative press and
sober citizens realize the absurdity of the Red Menace and the
hysteria was soon over." Chief Justice Earl Warren once remarked, "Of all the public services performed by Charles Evans
Hughes none was on a higher plane or called for more courage
than this. It was one of his finest hours in a long life of distinguished public service. It was not difficult for him to take such
stands. He did so instinctively. With him, justice, fair dealing,
tolerance and equality were not mere intellectual pursuits. They
represented spiritual values without which our institutions could
not survive." [1]

Happy as Hughes was in private practice, it was not long before public office beckoned again. From 1921 to 1925 he served
as Secretary of State under both Harding and Coolidge. His

[1] Speech in New York City on November 12, 1956 at annual meeting of
the National Conference of Christians and Jews, reprinted in A. Craig
Baird, (ed.) *Representative American Speeches: 1956-1957* (New York: H.
W. Wilson, 1957), pp. 138-139.

greatest achievement during those years was his leadership of
the Washington Conference that sought a drastic limitation of
naval armaments. Of course, the rise of dictatorships in Japan,
Germany, and Italy, eventually made it evident that disarmament
was a ghastly mistake. Yet Hughes' "performance proved to be
the most effective blow that was struck for peace between the
two great wars of this century. Since the conference effected the
only general reduction of armaments in the history of the world,
it will remain a challenge to statesmanship as long as big navies
and national rivalries exist." [1]

When Hughes resigned as Secretary of State in 1925 in order
to return to private practice and a much needed rest from official
duties, it was generally acknowledged that he had been one of
America's most eminent directors of foreign affairs. The passing
of years has not dimmed his stature. Still regarded as one of the
world's leading diplomats, he was elected judge of the Permanent
Court of International Justice in 1928. He resigned that post at
the age of sixty-eight to embark on another strenuous episode as
Chief Justice.

Hughes had not been eager to return to the Court. But when
Chief Justice Taft resigned because of ill health on February 3,
1930, President Hoover felt that Hughes was the logical choice
for the office. The bitter debate over his confirmation in the
Senate came, therefore, as a surprise to both Hoover and Hughes.
The Senate "liberals" argued that Hughes was too old for the
job, that he had damaged the image of the Court by resigning
in 1916 to run for President, and that he was a tool of the rich
corporations whom he had served so well as a practicing lawyer.
Most of the denunciations of Hughes revolved around the last
charge. In the heat of battle his early record as a crusading investigator and as a liberal Governor of New York was forgotten.
His concern for the protection of individual freedoms both as
Associate Justice and private citizen was also ignored. Instead

[1] Merlo J. Pusey, *op. cit.*, II, 522.

Hughes was pictured, along with Hoover and Taft, as a reaction-
ary conservative who was responsible, in part, for the great depression of the thirties.

Typical of the attacks on Hughes was the one made by George
W. Norris, the Republican progressive from Nebraska who opposed Hughes' nomination because:

No man in public life so exemplifies the influence of powerful combinations in the political and financial world. During his active practice
he has been associated with men of immense wealth and lived in an
atmosphere of luxury which can only come from immense fortunes
and great combinations. . . . It is only fair to say that the man who
lives this kind of a life, whose practice brings him wealthy clients and
monopolistic corporations seeking special governmental favor, it is
reasonable to expect that these influences have become a part of the
man. His viewpoint is clouded. He looks through glasses contaminated
by the influence of monopoly as it seeks to get favors by means which
are denied to the common, ordinary citizen.[1]

The debate over Hughes in the Senate continued through the
anniversary of Lincoln's birthday on February 12 and afforded
Senator Clarence Dill of Washington the opportunity to make
some unflattering comparisons. Lincoln was eulogized as the
"greatest champion of human rights in the world since Christ"
while Hughes was characterized as the "greatest champion of
property rights of our time. What a contrast the lives of these
two men present—Lincoln, the child of disappointment, poverty,
and sorrow, of whom it has been so truthfully said that when he
was 'entrusted with absolute power he never abused it, except
on the side of mercy,' and Hughes, the embodiment of culture,
good fortune, and worldly success, of whom it be equally truthfully said, 'property rights and great monopolies and the money
power in America never had an abler or a more effective champion.'"[2] In a concluding remark Senator Dill stated that, as

[1] *Congressional Record*, LXXII (1930), 3773.
[2] *Ibid.*, p. 3499.

Chief Justice, Hughes would "overturn and destroy practically everything" that Lincoln as well as Jefferson stood for because he had always been on the side of property rights.

Hughes was finally confirmed as Chief Justice by a vote of 52 to 26. It will be recalled from Chapter 1 that in the entire history of the Court only the nomination of Roger B. Taney to the highest judicial post had raised such a furor in the Senate. It has been well written that "the Senate's orgy on this occasion will never be fully explained, but certain aspects of it are understandable. America was in the first throes of the great depression of the thirties. The Insurgents were striking more at the Taft court and the Hoover Administration than at Hughes as an individual. For the moment Hughes was made an unwitting symbol of the philosophy which they believed to be responsible for the country's economic convulsions. The strange thing is that men who claimed to be 'liberals' chose as their target one of the greatest champions of human rights in the current century." [1] Perhaps further explanation for the vehement attack on Hughes may be found in his own words written on another occasion: "It is hard for some persons to understand that when a lawyer of the right sort takes a public place, he brings to the public the same loyalty and singleness of purpose that he displayed in his relations to his private clients." [2]

Hughes was Chief Justice during one of the most critical periods in American history—a period when the principle of judicial review was put to a severe test. It was a heavy burden that might easily have destroyed a less capable man. For Hughes it simply was another job to be done as efficiently and honestly as possible. As Justice Frankfurter has noted, Hughes "took his seat at the center of the Court, with a mastery that derived from his experience, as diversified, intense, and extensive, as any man ever brought to a seat on the Court, combined with a very powerful and acute mind that could mobilize these vast resources in the

[1] Merlo J. Pusey, *op. cit.*, II, 650-660.
[2] *Ibid.*, p. 637.

conduct of the business of the Court. . . . To see him preside was like witnessing Toscanini lead an orchestra." [1]

As usual, Hughes did everything well. He became an administrator of real distinction. The Court's docket was cleared. He assigned cases with skill and wisdom. "He never checked free debate, but the atmosphere which he created, the moral authority which he exerted, inhibited irrelevance, repetition, and fruitless discussion. He was a master of timing: he knew when discussion should be deferred and when brought to an issue." [2] Most important, Hughes was on warm and friendly terms with all the members of the Court. He had the ability to allay jealousies and minimize personal frictions. This was no mean accomplishment on a Court made up of strong, tough-minded personalities divided into conservative and liberal blocs.

Hughes' greatest test came when President Roosevelt proposed his famous "Court-packing bill" in February, 1937. Roosevelt asked Congress for authority to add a new justice to the Court whenever a member had failed to retire upon reaching the age of seventy. Since there were six justices over seventy on the Court at that time, the legislation would make it possible for the President to add six new judges of his own choosing. Roosevelt stated that new appointments were necessary because the Court was badly behind in its work and because men beyond seventy were too old to be judges. Of course, it was well known that Roosevelt's real reason was a desire to obtain a judicial approval of his New Deal program. The Court had already scuttled the heart of the Roosevelt program by invalidating such key legislation as the National Industrial Recovery Act, the Agricultural Adjustment Act, and the Frazier-Lemcke Act for the relief of farm mortgage debtors. Six Roosevelt appointees could easily reverse the "horse and buggy" Court.

Roosevelt's proposal caused a political storm of immense pro-

[1] Felix Frankfurter, *Of Law and Men* (New York: Harcourt, Brace, 1956), p. 133.
[2] *Ibid.*, p. 141.

portions. The Court became the center of a raging controversy. Hughes, sensing immediately that the future of the Court might well depend on the outcome of the struggle, moved cautiously and skillfully. Though singularly opposed to the Roosevelt scheme, he held his tongue and bided his time. Six weeks after the proposal was announced he noted publicly that the Court was "fully abreast of its work" with no congestion of cases on the calendar. He also raised some practical objections to enlarging the Court stating that an increase in the number of justices would impair rather than promote efficiency. Hughes never mentioned the differences over the New Deal legislation. But within a few weeks he led the Court to a new base by upholding key New Deal measures such as a new farm mortgage moratorium act and the Wagner National Labor Relations Act. Roosevelt no longer needed his Court-packing bill. The proposal was doomed. As one writer has aptly put it, "Hughes never retreated —he firmly advanced to the rear." He bowed gracefully to the political realities of the day and the pressure of changing times in a nonpolitical fashion to kill the Roosevelt proposal and maintain the power and dignity of the Court. "Without Marshall the court would not have attained its place in American life, without Hughes it might have lost that place. Marshall apart, Hughes is one of our greatest Chief Justices." [1]

As Chief Justice, Hughes also made major contributions to American civil liberties. To those who knew Hughes well this came as no surprise, for despite the vicious charges made by many "liberal" senators in 1930, Hughes never could be classified as liberal or conservative. He himself felt that such labels were largely meaningless. Perhaps the most that can be said is that Hughes "was decidedly liberal on issues of civil liberties and civil rights and moderately conservative on issues of social and economic reform."

Only a year after Hughes took office it became clear that a

---

[1] Zechariah Chafee, Jr., "Charles Evans Hughes," *Proceedings of the American Philosophical Society*, XCIII (1949), 281.

new era had dawned for American freedoms. Under his powerful influence the Court moved quickly to make freedom of speech
and thought, freedom of the press, freedom of religion and free
assembly "living law in the states as well as the nation." It was
evident that something new had happened. "What had been the
lonely views of Justices Holmes and Brandeis were becoming the
views of the majority of the Supreme Court." As early as 1934,
one student of the Court remarked aptly that Hughes had shown
"a greater fondness for the Bill of Rights than any Chief Justice
the country ever had."

Perhaps Hughes' most memorable opinion was his dissent in
United States v. *Macintosh* where he was joined by three of the
Court's most eminent men—Holmes, Brandeis, and Stone. Hughes'
dissent in that case gave dramatic proof of his humanitarianism,
and proved false the many who regarded him as the "greatest
champion of property rights," with no concern for human rights.

THE CASE

Clyde Macintosh was born in Ontario, Canada in 1877. He
graduated from MacMaster University in Toronto and came to
the United States in 1904 to take up graduate work at the University of Chicago. In 1907 Macintosh was ordained a Baptist
minister and returned to Canada to teach. Two years later he
went to Yale as professor of religion. Macintosh was eager to become an American citizen but World War I broke out just
as he had completed his five year residence requirement. He was
reluctant to renounce his British citizenship at the moment of
war. Instead, he volunteered for service as a Chaplain in the
Canadian Army. He served for two years in England and France,
seeing action near Vimy Ridge and in the Battle of the Somme.
He returned to the United States in 1917 to make a series of
public addresses in support of the Allies. The next year Macintosh was back in France as a volunteer in charge of an American

Y.M.C.A. hut at the front in the St. Mihiel region. He stayed in France until the end of the war when he resumed his teaching duties at Yale.

After the war, still anxious to become an American citizen, Macintosh applied for United States citizenship. An administrative tangle over the lack of documentary proof of his entry into the United States held up his application for a number of years. It was not until 1925 that he was able to file a declaration to become an American citizen. In 1929 his petition for naturalization was finally presented to the Federal District Court in New Haven, Connecticut. By that time Professor Macintosh was relatively well known for his contributions to religious and philosophical thought. A contemporary journal of religion described him as a person who "would never be mistaken for the president of a Rotary Club. Nature never designed him as a convention greeter. On the other hand, he would never come under the heading of the title of a recent book, 'God's Frozen Children.' Hundreds of students and a greater multitude of friends outside of the student ranks, have experienced the warmth of his friendship, his understanding sympathy and inspiring devotion." [1]

On the preliminary form for naturalization Macintosh was asked a series of questions designed to test his devotion to the principles of the Constitution. He was asked, in question number twenty, if he was willing to take the oath of allegiance. Macintosh replied, "Yes." But when asked in question number twenty-two if he would take up arms in defense of this country he qualified his answer. Macintosh responded, "Yes, but I should want to be free to judge as to the necessity." He subsequently filed a written memorandum explaining his position more fully to the Court.

I am willing to do what I judge to be in the best interests of my country, but only in so far as I can believe that this is not going to

[1] Halford E. Luccock, "Douglas Clyde Macintosh," *The Christian Century*, January 20, 1932, p. 89.

be against the best interests of humanity in the long run. I do not undertake to support "my country, right or wrong" in any dispute which may arise, and I am not willing to promise beforehand, and without knowing the cause for which my country may go to war, either that I will or that I will not "take up arms in defense of this country," however "necessary" the war may seem to be to the government of the day.

It is only in a sense consistent with these statements that I am willing to promise to "support and defend" the government of the United States "against all enemies, foreign and domestic." But, just because I am not certain that the language of questions 20 and 22 will bear the construction I should have to put upon it in order to be able to answer them in the affirmative, I have to say that I do not know that I can say "yes" in answer to these two questions.

At the hearing before the Federal District Court Macintosh gave a more detailed account of his position. He said that he was not a pacifist but felt that he could take up arms only if he believed that a war was morally justified. He was ready to give allegiance to the United States but he could not put allegiance to any country above the will of God. As an individual, Macintosh felt that he had the right to refrain from taking up arms in support of his government if a future war contravened what he understood to be the moral principles of Christianity.

The Federal District Court refused to grant citizenship to Macintosh because of his refusal to bear arms under any circumstance. In a brief holding the court stated that since Macintosh would not promise *in advance* to bear arms in defense of the United States, "he is not attached to the principles of the Constitution." Therefore, the court decreed that his "petition for citizenship is denied."

Stung by the decision of the District Court, Macintosh took his case to a Circuit Court of Appeals. In a unanimous decision the three-judge Court of Appeals reversed the lower court and ordered that Macintosh be admitted to citizenship. In its long opinion the Court of Appeals refused to be governed by the decision of the Supreme Court in *Schwimmer* v. *United States*. The court went to great lengths to show the distinction between the two cases.

The question presented here differs from that presented in the case of Schwimmer v United States. She stated she was an absolute atheist, and said, "I am not willing to bear arms," but she was willing to do everything that an American citizen must do except fight. This applicant was willing to bear arms and reserved the right to determine for himself whether the war was justified according to the dictates of his conscience.

Mrs. Schwimmer said she was an uncompromising pacifist, and was found to have no sense of nationalism, but only a cosmic sense of belonging to the human family, and opposed the use of military force as admitted by the Constitution and by the laws.

The appellant, on the other hand, was willing to give the United States "all the allegiance he ever had given or could give to any country," but said he would not put allegiance to the Government of any country before the will of God. This appellant, from his answers, indicates an upright sense of obligation to his God, and has carefully explained his willingness to be a citizen of the United States, assuming the responsibilities and obligations of its form of Government, and at the same time he has a high regard for his general duty to humanity. He wishes to keep pure his religious scruples.

The court of appeals noted further that it is recognized that a citizen has a duty to bear arms, "but there is also the well-recognized affection for his Government if, by reason of a conscientious religious scruple, he requests being excused from bearing arms. . . . There is a distinction between a morally justified and an unjustified war as recognized in international law. Such recognition was given in the recent Kellogg pact."

Despite the unanimous decision of the Court of Appeals the federal government decided to carry the case to the Supreme Court. Before the Court the Solicitor General of the United States argued that the oath of allegiance as required by the Naturalization Act must be taken without any qualifications or reservations whatsoever. Macintosh was represented by John W. Davis, a brilliant, conservative lawyer and unsuccessful Democratic Party candidate for President in 1924. Davis argued simply that the Naturalization Act did not require that his client promise in advance to bear arms in any future war.

In a five to four decision the Supreme Court, speaking through Justice George Sutherland, reversed the Court of Appeals and affirmed the judgment of the District Court denying Macintosh admission to citizenship. On the same day that the Macintosh case was decided, the Court also denied citizenship to Marie A. Bland, a Canadian nurse, who had also refused to swear without qualification that she would take up arms in defense of the United States.

Justice Sutherland was joined by Justices Van Devanter, McReynolds, Butler, and Roberts. In writing the majority opinion, Sutherland relied heavily on the Schwimmer case. He thought that Congress had clearly required an applicant for citizenship to promise to bear arms. He remarked, "It is not within the province of the courts to make bargains with those who seek naturalization. They must accept the grant and take the oath in accordance with the terms fixed by the law, or forego the privilege of citizenship. There is no middle choice. . . . The Naturalization Act is to be construed 'with definite purpose to favor and support the government,' and the United States is entitled to the benefit of any doubt which remains in the mind of the Court as to any essential matter of fact. The burden was upon the applicant to show that his views were not opposed to 'the principle that it is a duty of citizenship, by force of arms when necessary, to defend the country against all enemies, and that (his) opinions and beliefs would not prevent or impair the true faith and allegiance required by the act.' . . . We are of opinion that he did not meet this requirement."

Hughes dissented strongly. In his opening statement he remarked that the key question before the Court was whether or not Congress had required that a promise to bear arms was a necessary condition for naturalization. To him it was apparent that Congress had not made such an express requirement.

The question is whether that exaction is to be implied from certain general words which do not, as it seems to me, either literally or historically demand the implication. I think that the requirement should not be implied, because such construction is directly opposed to the spirit of our institutions and to the historic practice of the Congress. It must be conceded that departmental zeal may not be permitted to outrun the authority conferred by statute. If such a promise is to be demanded, contrary to principles which have been respected as fundamental, the Congress should exact it in unequivocal terms, and we should not, by judicial decision, attempt to perform what, as I see it, is a legislative function.

Hughes noted that the naturalization oath is the same, in substance, as the oath required for civil officers. He argued that Congress, in framing the oath for civil officers, did not intend to impose any religious test.

When we consider the history of the struggle for religious liberty, the large number of citizens of our country from the very beginning, who have been unwilling to sacrifice their religious convictions, and in particular, those who have been conscientiously opposed to war and who would not yield what they sincerely believed to be their allegiance to the will of God, I find it impossible to conclude that such persons are to be deemed disqualified for public office in this country because of the requirement of the oath which must be taken before they enter upon their duties. The terms of the promise "to support and defend the Constitution of the United States against all enemies, foreign and domestic" are not, I think to be read as demanding any such result. There are other and most important methods of defense, even in time of war, apart from the personal bearing of arms. . . . I think that the requirement of the oath of office should read in the light of our regard from the beginning for freedom of conscience.

Since Congress had reproduced the "historic words of the oath of office in the naturalization oath," it should be interpreted in the same way.

Hughes' most telling blows came in the latter part of his argument, where he revealed clearly his regard for the personal rights in the following passage.

Much has been said of the paramount duty to the State, a duty to be recognized, it is urged, even though it conflicts with convictions of a duty to God. Undoubtedly that duty to the State exists within the domain of power, for government may enforce obedience to laws regardless of scruples. When one's belief collides with the power of the State, the latter is supreme within its sphere and submission or punishment follows. But, in the forum of conscience, duty to a moral power higher than the State has always been maintained. The reservation of that supreme obligation, as a matter of principle, would unquestionably be made by many of our conscientious and law-abiding citizens. The essence of religion is belief in a relation to God involving duties superior to those arising from any human relation. . . . The battle for religious liberty has been fought and won with respect to religious beliefs and practices, which are not in conflict with good order, upon the very ground of the supremacy of conscience within its proper field. . . . There is abundant room for enforcing the requisite authority of law as it is enacted and requires obedience, and for maintaining the conception of the supremacy of law as essential to orderly government, without demanding that either citizens or applicants for citizenship shall assume by oath an obligation to regard allegiance to God as subordinate to allegiance to Civil power. The attempt to exact such a promise, and thus to bind one's conscience by the taking of oaths or the submission to tests, has been the cause of many deplorable conflicts. The Congress has sought to avoid such conflicts in this country by respecting our happy tradition. In no sphere of legislation has the intention to prevent such clashes been more conspicuous than in relation to the bearing of arms. It would require strong evidence that the Congress intended a reversal of its policy in prescribing the general terms of the Naturalization Oath. I find no such evidence.

The powerful dissenting opinion of the best-known Baptist layman in the country won wide support. The leading religious journals of every denomination praised Hughes' opinion and initiated a sustained assault on the Court's majority decision.

Resolutions were adopted by various religious organizations condemning the majority opinion. Both liberal and conservative newspapers and periodicals castigated the narrow view of the Court. A leading student of American civil liberties remarked aptly that "there is something humorous in the denial of American citizenship to persons of high intelligence, public spirit, and humanitarian sympathies like Douglas Macintosh and Rosika Schwimmer on the single ground of their unwillingness to bear arms, while during the same decade of Prohibition a considerable number of naturalized citizens were disturbing the country by their excessive willingness to bear arms, especially sawed-off shotguns and machine guns. A wise naturalization policy should not make everybody turn on a single opinion of the petitioner, especially when age or sex makes that opinion of little practical importance." [1]

On July 1, 1941, Chief Justice Hughes retired from the Court amid the plaudits of a grateful people. But though he was no longer on the bench, he lived to see his Macintosh dissent vindicated. On April 22, 1946—some two years before the death of Hughes—the Supreme Court overruled the Schwimmer and Macintosh cases in *Girouard* v. *United States*. Relying heavily on the dissents in those cases, the Court, speaking through Justice Douglas, granted citizenship to a Seventh Day Adventist who was willing to perform noncombatant duties in the Army but would not promise to bear arms because of his religious convictions. Agreeing fully with the Hughes dissent, Justice Douglas remarked that "there is not the slightest suggestion that Congress set a stricter standard for aliens seeking admission to citizenship than it did for officials who made and enforce the laws of the nation and administer its affairs. It is hard to believe that one need forsake his religious scruples to become a citizen but not to sit in the high councils of state."

[1] Zechariah Chafee Jr., *Free Speech in the United States* (Cambridge: Harvard University Press, 1942), p. 374.

In 1949 the Court granted citizenship to a man who refused to serve in the Army in *any* capacity on the authority of the Girouard Case. In 1950 and 1952 Congress provided that pacifists who base their refusal to bear arms on religious grounds may be naturalized. Hughes had finally prevailed!

VI

Justice Hugo Black
and *Chambers* v. *Florida*

*Of how a former Senator from Alabama, roundly denounced
for his previous membership in the Ku Klux Klan, came to
the defense of four friendless Negroes sentenced to death for
murder.*

THE MAN

WHEN HUGO LA FAYETTE BLACK became President Franklin
D. Roosevelt's first appointee to the Supreme Court in 1937,
there were few to applaud the selection. In fact, Black went to
the Supreme Court with a heavy handicap indeed. He was
roundly denounced by liberals as well as conservatives, fellow
senators, lawyers, and laymen who were appalled at the thought
that Black had once been a member of the Ku Klux Klan—an
organization whose opposition to Negroes, Roman Catholics, and
Jews was well known. The anti-Roosevelt *New York Herald
Tribune* of August 13, 1937, in a fairly typical comment, lamented
that Black's "record at the bar offers not the slightest qualification for the high office to which the President would elevate him."
The *Tribune* further argued that Black possessed "meager technical equipment" and that his appointment to the Court was a
"national tragedy."

Amidst all the shouting and furor Senator John Bankhead, Black's colleague from Alabama, rose on the Senate floor to defend the man who had once been his political enemy. "Let us all give him a chance to act upon that great Court," he said. "Let us wait and let history unfold its unwritten record." [1] Though the record is not yet complete there is no doubt that Black's detractors were very wrong indeed. Time has proven that perhaps "the most brilliant single stroke of the Roosevelt administration was the appointment of Hugo L. Black to the Supreme Court." [2] Today Justice Black stands as one of the foremost leaders of the Court and one of America's stanchest supporters of individual liberties. Many students of constitutional law already rank Black with the handful of truly great Supreme Court justices.

It has been well said that Justice Black "climbed to the heights rung by rung." Certainly no one would have picked Clay County, Alabama, where Black was born on a farm in 1886, as the ideal early training ground for a future Supreme Court justice. In those days Clay County was a backward, poverty-stricken, rural area. There was little opportunity for even a rudimentary education. All one's energies were needed to eke out a bare subsistence level livelihood from the poor, stubborn soil.

Black was the eighth and last child of Martha and William Black, ambitious parents who wanted to provide good educations for all their children. Hence, when Black was five years old, the family moved to Ashland, the County seat of Clay County, where there were better schools. Black's father opened a small general store and eventually became a fairly successful merchant. Meanwhile the children attended the local schools. Until he was sixteen, Black studied at a glorified private school called Ashland College, which has been described as a "primitive sort of academy." During these early years in Clay County, Black be-

[1] *Senate Misc. Documents,* 75th Congress, 1st Sess. (1937), no. 118, p. 9.
[2] Quoted in Charles A. Madison, "Justice Hugo Black: Still Dissenting at 70," *The Nation,* CLXXXII (January 25, 1956), 156.

came fascinated by politics and by the arguments of County lawyers in the Ashland Courthouse. He became known as a "courthouse pest for he dogged the country lawyers and soaked up their knowledge."

During these early years in Clay County, Black began to develop a point of view which he was to carry with him to the Supreme Court. In general he began to sympathize with the objectives of the Populists and liberal Democrats of his time.

The issue of free silver soon disappeared, but certain deep convictions about anti-trust laws, control of financial institutions, regulation of wealth through the income tax, and opposition to the intervention of courts in labor disputes became Black's fixed principles of political action. Of even deeper importance, Black drew from the agitation in Clay County strong sympathy based on the most intimate acquaintance with the very poor, and he became absolutely saturated with the essential conception of the Populist philosophy, that the people had the right through their government to improve the condition of their daily lives. When Black left Clay County, he took with him virtually nothing in the way of wealth and education; but he carried the general purpose of those who in later decades were called New Dealers.[1]

Black had always been interested in law, but at the age of seventeen he enrolled in the Birmingham Medical College largely to please his mother and older brother who was already a doctor. A year of medical training convinced Black that he still wanted to be a lawyer. He left the medical school and at eighteen entered the University of Alabama Law School without any college training. But he worked hard, completed the two-year law program with honors in 1906, and was admitted to the bar.

Black returned to Ashland and started to practice law in a small second-floor office above a grocery store. He spent all the money he had on a library, and then waited for his clients to appear. There were few clients and even less money. To make

[1] John P. Frank, *Mr. Justice Black: The Man and His Opinions* (New York: A. A. Knopf, 1949), pp. 11-12. Reprinted by permission.

matters worse, the building containing his office soon burned
to the ground. His entire library was lost in the fire. With less
than $10.00 in his pocket Black left Ashland to seek his fortune
in Birmingham, "the Pittsburgh of the South."

Black worked hard at the difficult task of acquiring a practice
in Birmingham. "The story of his experiences as a young lawyer
trying to get started sound like pages out of Horatio Alger's
books. He lived in boarding houses with four men in a room and
he got desk space wherever he could find it in some law office
downtown. Things got so bad that when an insurance company
in Atlanta sent him a few dollars' worth of business, he looked
upon it as a life saver." [1] But Black was persistent and his reputation as an honest, thorough, tough-minded but compassionate
trial lawyer grew. Unlike most successful lawyers in Birmingham
who served the banks, power companies, and large corporations,
Black built his practice among the trade unions, farmers, and
Negroes. In short, he became a strong spokesman for the under-
privileged. During this period he also served as a police court
judge, for eighteen months spending his mornings in a "hot,
dingy courtroom disposing of defendants, mostly Negro, hauled
in for shooting craps, loafing, fighting and connubial incom-
patibility." [2] Extensive newspaper coverage of Black's cases
helped to make him a well-known figure in Birmingham.

In 1914 Black was elected county prosecuting attorney and
proceeded to take militant action against bootleg and gambling
rings. He enforced the law just as vigorously against entrenched
local interests such as coal and insurance companies. In addition,
Black launched an investigation which put a stop to the third-
degree methods used against Negroes by the police in the town
of Bessemer, a suburb of Birmingham. The Bessemer police had

---

[1] James S. Childers, "Hugo Black, Always an Alabamian," *The Birmingham News–Age–Herald,* January 31, 1937, p. 3.

[2] Raymond Clapper, "Hugo Black—Nemesis of Subsidy Spoilsmen," *Review of Reviews,* April, 1934, p. 19.

been obtaining confessions by beating Negroes with sticks, chairs, leather straps, and anything else they could obtain "until they were red with their own blood."

Black's legal career was interrupted for a year when he volunteered for service in the Army in 1917. He never served outside the United States, was discharged as an artillery captain and returned to Birmingham to resume his law practice. In 1921 he married Josephine Foster, daughter of a Presbyterian minister. Black joined a number of organizations such as the Mason's, Odd Fellows, and Moose. His practice began to boom. In 1923 Black joined the Birmingham chapter of the Ku Klux Klan largely as a matter of political expediency. He remained a member of the Klan for almost two years, resigning in 1925 when he decided to run for the United States Senate.

Black was completely free of the racial and religious prejudices which have long been associated with the Ku Klux Klan. Why, then, did he join the organization? Perhaps the best explanation has been given by his biographer and admirer, who has pointed out that Black deliberated for almost a year before joining the Klan.

The reasons for staying out were the obvious ones—he had very close friends among the groups that some Klansmen condemned; he had consistently and publicly upheld fair play for Negroes; he had never in his life given evidence to anyone of a belief that Nordics had a right to rule the world. The reasons for joining were also simple: he was a poor man's lawyer, and thousands of Birmingham workmen were in the Klan; and he was ambitious for political advancement. The rationalizations were three-fold: first, that very few Klan members either practiced or approved of racial violence; second, that perhaps there was a chance to bore for decency from within; and third, that the Southern liberal in politics must do a certain amount of pretending if he is to stay in politics at all.[1]

Black seemed to have little hope of going to the United States Senate in 1926, since there were four other candidates in the

[1] John P. Frank, *op. cit.*, p. 38.

race—all with more experience and money, and better known throughout the state. But Black conducted a hard, tireless campaign. For thirteen months he traveled into every town and county of the state, meeting and talking to people. With the support of organized labor, small farmers, prohibitionists and the Ku Klux Klan, Black won a resounding victory. In 1927 he arrived in Washington to take his seat in the Republican dominated Senate.

Black had no illusions about his qualifications for the Senate. He knew he had much to learn. Unlike many freshmen politicians, Black talked very little during his first year in Washington. Instead he spent much of his time observing, listening and reading. He became thoroughly familiar with Senate rules and began a systematic program of reading in history, economics, philosophy and government. By the end of the term he had emerged as a hard-working, skilled parliamentarian and a militant liberal. Re-elected in 1932, Black sponsored and supported many important New Deal measures, including the Fair Standards Labor Act and the Tennessee Valley Authority. He also conducted a series of major investigations into lobbying activities, ship subsidies, and trusts. In 1936 he campaigned vigorously for the re-election of President Roosevelt.

Black also gave strong support to Roosevelt's Court-packing bill, which would have added up to six new justices to the Court and made possible the judicial approval of the New Deal. The "nine old men" had already destroyed the heart of the Roosevelt program by holding to be unconstitutional eight out of ten New Deal measures. The Court-packing bill was roundly defeated, but from 1937 to 1941 death and retirements enabled Roosevelt to appoint seven justices who sympathized with the New Deal. As noted above, the first of these was Hugo L. Black, a stanch New Dealer and perhaps the most radical man in the Senate. "The conservative Democrats and Republicans could not have been more horrified to learn that Satan himself had been appointed to the High Court. . . . No record shows exactly why the President

appointed Black. That he considered Black an able and ardent
New Dealer is clear. How much he was influenced by two related considerations is not known: that the Senate could not
possibly fail to confirm one of its members, and that the appointment of one of the stoutest Roosevelt followers in the Senate was
bound to leave the majority, which had just defeated Roosevelt
[his Court-packing bill], in the state of frustrated fury." [1] But
Black's nomination was easily confirmed by the Senate. He took
the Oath of Office and with his family sailed to Europe for a brief
vacation.

On September 13, 1937, while Black was still in Europe, the
Pittsburgh Post-Gazette, in a series of six articles, revealed his
early connection with the Ku Klux Klan and maintained that he
was still a member. The articles created a national sensation.
Black's association with the Klan became headline news through-
out.the country. He was vilified by newspapers everywhere. The
National Association for the Advancement of Colored People
urged that he resign unless he could prove that the charges were
false. Roman Catholic groups throughout the country demanded
that he resign or suffer impeachment. In Europe, Black was be-
sieged by reporters asking for a statement. He refused to say anything until he returned home.

On October 1, 1937, Black delivered an eleven-minute radio
address from Chevy Chase, Maryland, to a nationwide audience
of some fifty million—one of the largest audiences ever to hear
a radio speech. He minced no words. "My words and acts are a
matter of public record," he said.

I believe that my record as a Senator refutes every implication of racial
and religious intolerance. It shows that I was of that group of liberal
Senators who have consistently fought for the civil, economic, and religious rights of all Americans without regard to race or creed. The
insinuations of racial and religious intolerance made concerning me
are based on the fact that I joined the Ku Klux Klan about fifteen
years ago. I did join the Klan. I later resigned. I never rejoined. . . . I

[1] John P. Frank, *op. cit.,* p. 98.

have never considered and I do not now consider the unsolicited card given to me shortly after my nomination to the Senate as a membership of any kind in the Ku Klux Klan. I never used it. I did not even keep it. Before becoming a Senator I dropped the Klan. I have had nothing to do with it since that time. . . . I have among my friends many members of the colored race. I have watched the progress of its members with sympathy and admiration. Certainly they are entitled to the full measure of protection accorded to the citizenship of our country by the Constitution and our laws.[1]

Three days after his radio address Black sat as a member of the Court for the first time. The uproar over his membership in the Klan gradually died down. Black's connection with the Klan was indeed unfortunate and his defense not entirely adequate. Writing in 1961, Norman Thomas, who had opposed Black's elevation to the Court said: "I see no reason for repentance that I was one of those opposed to his appointment; only satisfaction that our reasonable fears were so handsomely allayed by time." Justice Black himself has always believed that the furor over his appointment "was really occasioned not by dislike of his past membership in the K.K.K. but dislike of his radical economic views." [2] He is still somewhat embittered toward newspapers for their part in the attack.

Black went to the Court as an expert legislator but with little judicial experience and a limited knowledge of constitutional law. But through incessant hard work and study he soon became a strong and distinguished justice. His opinions are characterized by simplicity of style and clarity. As one of the most vigorous supporters of civil rights in the history of the Court, he has failed to vote for the protection of basic civil rights in only a few instances. He has been severely criticized for his opinion in *Korematsu* v. *United States,* discussed in Chapter 7, upholding the compulsory evacuation of persons of Japanese ancestry from the

[1] *The New York Times,* October 2, 1937. Copyright by *The New York Times.* Reprinted by permission.

[2] Anthony Lewis, "Justice Black at 75: Still the Dissenter," *The New York Times Magazine,* February 26, 1961, p. 74.

West Coast during World War II. He felt, at that time, that the
military denial of individual freedom was justified by the emergency. It was also a surprise to find him with the majority in the
Yamashita case, discussed in Chapter 8. Nevertheless, few justices have been more passionate spokesmen for civil liberties. In
general, Justice Black has preached the doctrine that "government should at the same time be both all-powerful and all weak:
that over the economy it should have all the power needed to
cope with the problems of each day, and that over the thought,
speech and spirit of the citizen it should have no power at all." [1]

On the Warren Court, Black is the acknowledged leader of the
"judicial activists" who believe that they must play a positive
role in the protection of individual liberties. This group seeks to
promote social welfare and protect American freedoms from
erosion by partisan legislatures and executive officers. Black sees
the Court as the ultimate guardian of constitutional rights. Justice
Felix Frankfurter, on the other hand, who retired in 1962, advocated a policy of "judicial self-restraint." He and his supporters
believe that the primary responsibility for governing lies with
the people and their duly elected officers. The Frankfurter view
was that the basic dilemmas of our society must be resolved by
legislatures "lest the freedom of the people to govern themselves,
well or badly be hampered by 'judicial legislation.'"

Of course, neither of these views has wholly prevailed, but
Black's bold stand may have done more to remind Americans of
their precious heritage than anything else that has occurred in
the twentieth century. For Black the prohibitions of the Constitution are not "mere admonitions" that need not always be observed. They are "absolutes" that must be strictly enforced by
the Court. Thus Black is the dedicated idealist, in search of the
illusive American dream, who uses the power of judicial review
to support the weak, the poor, the needy and the downtrodden.
Perhaps none of Black's opinions better demonstrates his zeal

[1] John P. Frank, "Mr. Justice Black: A Biographical Appreciation," *Yale
Law Journal*, LXV (1956), 461.

for individual freedom than that in *Chambers* v. *Florida*, written
when he had been on the Court less than three years. Perhaps
Black's prose in this case does not have "the grace of Holmes' nor
the glow of Brandeis'." But in the words of the late famous historian, Charles A. Beard, Black's opinion in *Chambers* v. *Florida*
"will ring with power as long as liberty and justice are cherished
in our country. The whole document ought to be read by all
citizens who care for the perpetuity of the Republic." [1]

THE CASE

It was indeed a dastardly crime—one that would arouse the ire
of any community. It happened on a warm Saturday night—May
13, 1933—in Pompona, Florida, a small town in Broward County,
about twelve miles from Fort Lauderdale, the county seat.
Around nine o'clock, Robert Darcy, an elderly white man, closed
his fish market and started for home. He never made it. On the
way he was beaten, robbed, and left to die on the roadway. The
body was found around nine-thirty the same evening. Within
the next twenty-four hours a number of Negroes living in the
vicinity were arrested without warrants as suspects and confined
in the county jail at Fort Lauderdale. Among the Negroes arrested were Isiah Chambers, Jack Williamson, Charlie Davis,
and Walter Woodward—all poor, uneducated migratory farm
laborers who had recently arrived in the community.

On Sunday afternoon, May 14, the four prisoners and other
Negroes were questioned about the murder robbery by the
newly-elected county sheriff, a convict guard, and several other
white men. The questioning and cross-questioning continued
for a week without results. All the Negroes said over and over
again that they had nothing to do with the crime. During this
period the prisoners were not allowed to see any friends and

[1] Charles Beard, *The Republic* (New York: Viking Press, 1943), pp.
239-240.

relatives or to confer with a lawyer. They subsequently charged
that during the week they were continually threatened, cursed,
beaten, and tortured by the convict guard and other white men.
All of this was denied by the convict guard and the other ques-
tioners. In any event, by Saturday, May 20, after a week of persistent questioning, none of the Negroes had confessed to the
crime. But beginning about 3:30 P.M. on Saturday each prisoner
was questioned separately on and off all night long with no rest,
food, or opportunity for sleep. The prisoners also later claimed
that they were whipped and tortured at various intervals during
the night. This was also denied by the police officers. About
2:30 A.M. one of the prisoners—Walter Woodward, a very light-
skinned person, easy to sulk and down on the world—"broke"
and "confessed" to the crime. The state's attorney was called to
the jail to hear the confession but he would not accept it. He
told the sheriff and other police officers that they did not have
enough evidence and not to call him again until the confession
was more detailed.

The questioning continued until 6:00 A.M. when "something
worthwhile" was obtained. The state's attorney was called again.
This time Williamson, Davis, and Woodward confessed to the
crime. Before these confessions were made no formal charges
against the four Negroes had been entered. But two days after
the confessions the three men along with Chambers were indicted and arraigned. Chambers' indictment rested on the confessions of the other three men. One of the prisoners later testified that after the confessions had been obtained, the county
sheriff dangled a bunch of keys before the defendants' eyes and
told them to stick to the confessions or the keys would be turned
over to a crowd outside the jail waiting to lynch them.

The trial was held in the Broward County Circuit Court. The
presiding judge never issued a formal order appointing counsel
for the defendants, but he did ask two local lawyers to defend
them. The two lawyers did nothing. During the trial they made
no inquiries and asked no questions concerning the confessions

relied upon by the state to convict all of the accused. The four defendants—uneducated, with no knowledge whatsoever of their rights—did not know they were represented by counsel until June 17, 1933, the day they were all sentenced to death for the murder of Darcy.

Death Warrants for the execution of the condemned men were issued. They were about to be executed when the case went to the Florida Supreme Court for review. The Court had before it only the record of the prosecuting attorney since counsel for the defendants did not submit a brief or present arguments in their behalf. Nevertheless, the Florida Supreme Court on December 19, 1933, upheld the convictions stating that "nothing has been found in the transcript to raise the slightest doubt as to the propriety of the convictions and sentences in this case."

The case was destined to reach the Florida Supreme Court four more times during the next six years, largely through the efforts of Mr. S. D. McGill, an able and conscientious Negro attorney from Jacksonville, Florida, who had been outraged by the denial of fundamental rights. With the help of the National Association for the Advancement of Colored People, which raised some money for expenses, McGill fought a hard, long, and bitter battle.

In January, 1934, the state Supreme Court granted leave to present a petition for a new trial to the County Court on the basis that the judgments would have been different if the local Court had known that the confessions had not been voluntarily obtained. The trial court, however, denied the petition without considering the issues raised by the higher court. Late in 1934, the state Supreme Court reversed the trial court and ordered it to submit the issues to a jury. A new trial was held but the jury upheld the original convictions after finding that the charges of coercion in obtaining the confessions were not true. But again the Florida Supreme Court reversed, holding that the issue alleging that the confessions and pleas "were not in fact freely and voluntarily made" had not been clearly submitted to the jury. The Court stated that the "state's own evidence in this case strongly tends to the conclusion that these confessions were not in fact freely and voluntarily made, and were not 'the spontaneous expressions by these petitioners of their own guilt,' and this should have been clearly submitted to the jury for its determination."

After the fourth appeal a motion for change of venue by the defendants was granted and the case was transferred to West Palm Beach County for trial. Again the trial court found that the confessions were not coerced and that each of the defendants was guilty as charged. This time the Florida Supreme Court, on March 3, 1939, affirmed the convictions after noting that the confessions were voluntarily made. Only one judge—Joel B. Brown—dissented, saying as follows:

It may be that these four petitioners are in fact all guilty, and that they would be so found by a jury if this case should be remanded for a trial on the merits, without the confessions being introduced in evidence. But the guilt or innocence of these petitioners is not the question before us. The question here is whether, on the testimony, the verdict of the jury, finding in effect, that the confessions and pleas of guilty of these petitioners were freely and voluntarily made, should have been set aside by the trial judge on motion for a new trial.

My view is that the verdict of the jury was contrary to the weight and probative force of the evidence on this point, and the court below should have granted the motion for a new trial.

But in this instance I have based my conclusion upon the testimony of the State's witnesses alone. Taking the facts established by the State's own testimony, considered in the light of the applicable principles of law, my conclusion is that these confessions and pleas were not 'freely and voluntarily made.'

Despite the lone dissenting opinion the door was closed to any further appeals through the state courts. Only an appeal to the United States Supreme Court could now save the condemned men. Through their lawyers the four Negro defendants applied to the highest court for relief as paupers. The Supreme Court agreed to take the case and on January 4, 1940, arguments were heard. Appropriately enough on Lincoln's birthday, February

12, 1940, a unanimous Court, in a landmark decision, held that the confessions were illegally obtained and reversed the judgment of the Florida Supreme Court. The opinion of the Court was written by Justice Hugo L. Black, the southerner and former Klansman who had recently been so roundly denounced. By all odds, Black's opinion is the most celebrated of his early civil rights pronouncements, and perhaps will stand as his greatest monument to the cause of freedom.

Black was not content simply to reverse the convictions. With seldom matched eloquence he took the opportunity to assert great American principles of individual freedom. After reviewing the record of the case, Black noted that the due process clause of the Fourteenth Amendment was designed:

to protect, at all times, people charged with or suspected of crime by those holding positions of power and authority. The determination to preserve an accused's right to procedural due process sprang in large part from knowledge of the historical truth that the rights and liberties of people accused of crime could not be safely entrusted to secret inquisitorial processes. The testimony of centuries, in governments of varying kinds over populations of different races and beliefs, stood as proof that physical and mental torture and coercion had brought about the tragically unjust sacrifices of some who were the noblest and mose useful of their generations. The rack, the thumbscrew, the wheel, solitary confinement, protracted questioning and cross-questioning, and other ingenious forms of entrapment of the helpless or unpopular had left their wake of mutilated bodies and shattered minds along the way to the cross, the guillotine, the stake and the hangman's noose. And they who have suffered most from secret and dictatorial proceedings have almost always been the poor, the ignorant, the numerically weak, the friendless, and the powerless. . . .

Black then referred specifically to the record of the case that clearly "shows, without conflict, the dragnet methods of arrest on suspicion without warrant, and the protracted questioning and cross questioning of these ignorant young colored tenant farmers by state officers and other white citizens, in a fourth floor jail room, where as prisoners they were without friends, advisers, or counselors, and under circumstances calculated to break the strongest nerves and the stoutest resistance."

Black noted that for five days the Negroes

were subjected to interrogation culminating in Saturday's [May 20th] all night examination. Over a period of five days they steadily refused to confess and disclaimed any guilt. The very circumstances surrounding their confinement and their questioning without any formal charges having been brought, were such as to fill petitioners with terror and frightful misgivings. Some were practical strangers in the community; three were arrested in a one-room farm tenant-house which was their home; the haunting fear of mob violence was around them in an atmosphere charged with excitement and public indignation. From virtually the moment of their arrest until their eventual confessions, they never knew just when any one would be called back to the fourth floor room, and there, surrounded by accusers and others, interrogated by men who held their very lives—so far as these ignorant petitioners could know—in the balance. The rejection of petitioner Woodward's first "confession," given in the early hours of Saturday morning, because it was found wanting, demonstrates the relentless tenacity which "broke" petitioners' will and rendered them helpless to resist their accusers further. To permit human lives to be forfeited upon confessions thus obtained would make of the constitutional requirement of due process of law a meaningless symbol.

Justice Black's often quoted concluding remarks reveal clearly his legal credo. "We are not impressed by the argument that law enforcement methods such as those under review are necessary to uphold our laws," he said.

The Constitution proscribes such lawless means irrespective of the end. And this argument flouts the basic principle that all people must stand on an equality before the bar of justice in every American court. . . . Under our constitutional system, courts stand against any winds that blow as havens of refuge for those who might otherwise suffer because they are helpless, weak, outnumbered or because they are non-conforming victims of prejudice and public excitement. Due process of law, preserved for all by our Constitution, commands that no such practice as that disclosed by this record shall send any accused to his death. No higher duty, no more solemn responsibility, rests upon this Court, than that of translating into living law and maintaining this constitutional shield deliberately planned and inscribed for the benefit of every human being subject to our Constitution—of whatever race, creed or persuasion.

Black's opinion won him new friends and stilled the doubts of those who had feared his southern background and his Klan connections. Many who had attacked him unmercifully in 1937 now heaped praise on him for the decision. One publication, which had previously attacked Black's appointment to the Court, referred to the Chambers decision as "far and away the most direct, sweeping, and brilliantly written application of the Fourteenth Amendment to human rights that has come from our highest court." [1] The Chambers case is now embedded deeply in our constitutional law. It has become an important precedent—a warning to police officers everywhere that the highest court in the land will not tolerate coerced confessions. With this case Black established himself beyond doubt as a "vigorous and valiant interpreter of the Constitution," a man to be reckoned with and listened to.

BACK TO FLORIDA

After the Supreme Court decision the case was returned to Florida where the trial court, as directed, threw out the confessions. This left the trial court with insufficient evidence for a new trial, since without the confessions the only evidence available was a bloody stick found in the yard where the defendants had lived and some indication that they had been in the neighborhood where the crime was committed. Furthermore, each of the defendants had for years steadfastly denied any knowledge of

[1] John A. Ryan, "Due Process and Mr. Justice Black," *Catholic World,* April, 1940, p. 38.

the crime. The trial court therefore directed a verdict of not guilty against the four defendants.

For Isiah Chambers, a very serious minded young man who brooded a great deal while in jail, it was indeed a hollow victory. A few years after the original trial he had been adjudged insane and confined in a Florida state hospital. The other three defendants—Jack Williamson, the most studious and best read of the group; Charlie Davis, a jolly, heavyset man who was an excellent singer; and Walter Woodward, the light-skinned Negro— were released from prison. They had been in jail for almost eight years. During this period they had only one visit from a relative —Walter Woodward's sister who came from South Carolina to see the prisoners and talk with their lawyers. One of the defense attorneys and a local Negro organization collected enough money to send the three men back to their original homes. They were never heard from again.

VII

Justice Frank Murphy
and *Korematsu* v. *United States*

*Of how the most underestimated Supreme Court Justice of
our time passionately defended the rights of Japanese-Americans forced from their homes during World War II.*

THE MAN

IN THE LONG HISTORY of the Supreme Court no justice has been
as passionately devoted to the protection of American individual
liberties as has Justice Murphy. He was willing to go further than
any other justice to defend human rights under the Constitution.
"Time and again he spoke eloquently on behalf of the constitutional and legal rights of the accused, the unpopular, and the op-
pressed. Sometimes he spoke on behalf of the Court, sometimes
for a minority of the Court, and not infrequently he spoke alone.
But always he reflected a humane and an understanding sense of
justice." [1] One of Murphy's warmest admirers has stated well
that the late Justice was the embodiment of the "persistent American ideal of human justice. He consistently and with effective
prose, sought to establish or to reinforce in American law basic

[1] "Proceedings in the Supreme Court in Memory of Mr. Justice Murphy,"
(1950), 340 U. S. XII.

constitutional principles of human freedom, and basic principles of social justice." [1]

Ironically enough, it was Murphy's sensitive concern for individual freedom that contributed to making him a controversial judicial figure. While Murphy's supporters maintain that he was an outstanding judge and the most underrated member of the Court in our time, others view him as a "legal illiterate" and "judicial misfit" who relied on his own compassionate instincts rather than on sound legal principles in deciding cases. It has been said that he was one of the "tender" justices whose "hearts were prone to dominate their heads." Murphy's detractors further maintain that his approach to law was too simple, too unorthodox. They argue that Murphy was a misplaced crusader rather than a legal craftsman with an appreciation for legal refinements. Though it is still too early to render final judgment, this much, at least, is clear: Murphy was a courageous, conscientious judge of little sophistication or pretense who "gave to the Court one of its finest hours of humanitarian justice." [2]

In retrospect it appears that Murphy was preparing all his life to become the Court's eloquent spokesman for individual freedom. Born in Harbor Beach, Michigan, a small town on Lake Huron, on April 13, 1890, Murphy was deeply influenced by his Irish, Roman Catholic parents. Murphy's father, an able lawyer and Democrat in a predominantly Republican community, was proud of his Irish revolutionary heritage. One of his ancestors had been hanged by the British for revolutionary activities. At sixteen he himself had been imprisoned in Canada for taking part in Fenian disturbances. He passed this spirit of independence and a passionate interest in politics on to his son. In addition, the elder Murphy instilled in his son a great love for the American system of government, which he viewed as the best hope of mankind.

[1] John P. Frank, "Justice Murphy: The Goals Attempted," *Yale Law Journal*, LI (December, 1949), 26.
[2] Eugene Gressman, "The Controversial Image of Mr. Justice Murphy," *Georgetown Law Journal*, XLVII (Summer, 1959), 654.

A devout Roman Catholic who hoped her son would become a priest, Murphy's mother was chiefly responsible for the deep religious conviction which never wavered throughout his life. At the same time, Murphy's mother taught him to respect the beliefs of other religious faiths. She impressed upon him a need to respect the rights of other minority groups, particularly Jews and Negroes. Most important, Mary Murphy fired her son with an intense ambition to succeed and better the lot of humanity. She implanted in her son "a sense of personal destiny and a moral code he never lost. In guiding his religious education, she instilled in him the ancient ideal that man is his brother's keeper, that salvation lies in good works, all leading to the conviction that the 'most precious virtue of all is the desire to serve mankind.' An avowedly idealistic standard, it was derived from the implicit premise that all individuals, and especially the strong, bear a responsibility for alleviating the suffering of the weak." [1]

Endowed with proverbial Irish wit and charm, Murphy, as his father had, entered the University of Michigan to study law. He was not a brilliant student. He seemed to be more interested in athletics and social affairs. But at Michigan Murphy did develop oratorical skills, which were of great help in his public career. In fact, he later emerged as one of the most eminent public speakers of his time—a man who "could and did bring men to their feet." After obtaining his undergraduate degree in 1912, Murphy spent the summer making speeches for his idol, Woodrow Wilson. Two years later he graduated from law school and went to work as a five-dollar-a-week law clerk for a prominent Detroit firm. To supplement his small income he lectured in a local law school and taught English to Hungarian immigrants three nights a week.

During his early years in Detroit Murphy became acquainted with many local Democratic politicians. He learned much about practical politics, but before he could actively participate the

[1] Howard J. Woodford, Jr., "Frank Murphy: A Liberal's Creed," (Unpublished Ph. D. dissertation, Department of Politics, Princeton University, 1959). C. 1.

United States entered the war in Europe. Murphy joined the Army, served in France and Germany, and became a captain. Upon his discharge he spent a year studying law at Lincoln's Inn, London and Trinity College, Dublin, where he renewed his sympathetic interest in the cause of Irish independence.

Murphy returned to Detroit in 1919 eager to enter politics and "imbued with a sense of personal destiny." He served for a year as an assistant United States district attorney and established a record of winning important cases. He resumed private practice but returned to public service in 1923 when he was elected to the Recorder's Court of Detroit, a criminal tribunal. It was while sitting as trial judge in the celebrated Sweet case in this court that Murphy first came to public notice.

The Sweet case grew out of the bitter racial tensions that had developed in Detroit after the war. A large number of Negroes from the South had migrated to Detroit to take jobs in the booming automobile industry. Housing in the already crowded Negro sections of the city was terribly inadequate. As a result many Negroes sought homes in white neighborhoods. Dr. Ossian H. Sweet, a Negro physician, bought a house in a previously all-white neighborhood. Shortly after he moved in a threatening mob of over 700 people gathered near his home. Shouts rang out. The mob flung stones at the house and windows were broken. Suddenly, shots were fired from one of the windows of the Sweet house. One white man in the mob was killed and another wounded. Dr. Sweet and ten other relatives and friends in the house with him were immediately arrested and charged with first degree murder. In this tense, inflamed atmosphere Murphy presided over the trial with dignity and impartiality.

Refusing to be intimidated by the public clamor and criticism he conducted the trial with scrupulous fairness to all concerned. The key Negro defendant was acquitted after a magnificent final seven hour plea to the jury by Clarence Darrow who argued that his Negro clients acted in self-defense. Murphy won high praise from Darrow for his conduct of the Sweet case. The famous lawyer later described Murphy as "a judge who not only seemed human, but who proved to be the kindliest and most understanding man I have ever happened to meet on the bench."

In 1929 Murphy was re-elected to the Recorder's Court but resigned a year later to run for mayor of Detroit. With the solid support of Irish-Americans, Negroes, and other minority groups, Murphy was elected Mayor just as the economic depression all but immobilized the city. He burst into national prominence with his statement that "not one deserving man or woman shall go hungry in Detroit because of circumstances beyond his control." Murphy was true to his word. He spent enormous sums on a massive public relief program for the unemployed in order to fulfill his pledge. At the same time he boldly called for federal public works programs and other forms of direct federal assistance to municipalities. In 1931 he was easily re-elected mayor.

In 1931 Murphy emerged as one of the original supporters of Franklin D. Roosevelt. Though a stanch Roman Catholic, he preferred Roosevelt to Alfred E. Smith. Murphy campaigned actively for Roosevelt, who shortly after entering the White House, rewarded him with the post of Governor General of the Philippine Islands. After the Commonwealth Government was established in 1935, Murphy remained in Manila as the first United States High Commissioner. He was sympathetic to the Filipinos' desire for independence and poured all his energies into improving conditions in the islands. Among other things, Murphy improved public health services and hospitals. An eight-hour day for industrial workers was begun. The fiscal affairs of the country were put in good order. When Murphy was drafted to run for Governor of Michigan in 1936, the Filipinos were truly dismayed to see the man they had come to love leave his post.

Murphy was elected governor and was immediately confronted with another crisis: the famous sit-down strikes in the automobile industry. Abhorring the use of violence, he refused to use troops to drive the workers from the factories. Instead, he held numerous conferences with union leaders and management representa-

tives until a peaceful settlement was reached. Murphy was
lauded in many quarters for settling the dispute without blood-
shed, but most business leaders condemned him bitterly as an
enemy of private property for refusing to oust the strikers by
force. As a result he was decisively defeated for re-election as
Governor in 1938.

Immediately after his defeat in Michigan, President Roosevelt
appointed Murphy Attorney General of the United States. In that
post Murphy antagonized a number of people because of his
seemingly "irresistable passion for publicity. Twice a week he
held press conferences, which were better attended than any in
Washington except those of the President." But Murphy accomplished much during his year as Attorney General. He vigorously
prosecuted corrupt local politicians who were members of his
own party. The Department of Justice was reorganized. Notable
men rather than political hacks were recommended to fill vacant
judgeships. Most important, within a month after taking office
Murphy established a Civil Rights Section in the Criminal Division of the Department of Justice to prosecute violators of federal civil rights statutes. Through the years the Civil Rights Section has become increasingly more active in helping individuals
whose personal liberties have been violated.

In 1940 President Roosevelt named Murphy Associate Justice
of the Supreme Court to fill the vacancy caused by the death of
the conservative Pierce Butler. Murphy, who remained a bachelor
all his life, served on the Court until his death in 1949. During
that relatively brief span of time he made it clear in opinion
after opinion that, for him, the protection of individual liberties
was the Court's most important function. "Eloquently, unasham-
edly and consistently," he gave his support to basic constitutional
principles of human freedom and basic precepts of economic and
social justice. To Murphy the constitution was "something more
than a restriction on the functions of the Court. It was also the
embodiment of the basic ideals and standards to which this nation is dedicated. It imposed upon the Court, no less than upon

and *Korematsu* v. *United States*

the President, the Congress, and the various state a[
duty of giving effect to those ideals and standards. .
that the constitutional guarantees of human freedoı
too important to be ignored by the Court on slight pretense.[1]

It has been well written that "Murphy's entire career illustrates
what happens when a passionate man of affairs takes the American creed seriously and attempts to apply ancient principles to
the solution of contemporary problems." [2] As a member of the
Court Murphy was willing to apply these ancient principles of
justice to all men regardless of race, color or creed. Perhaps nowhere is this better demonstrated than in his dissents in the
Yamashita Case discussed in Chapter 8 and in *Korematsu* v.
United States. Though Murphy cherished his Yamashita opinion
above all others, his Korematsu dissent was no less impassioned
or clear in meaning. Shortly after reading the entire Korematsu
decision, Norman Thomas aptly wrote to Murphy that "if
America is to continue and to grow as a democracy, I believe
your dissenting opinion will live as one of that democracy's great
documents. You have put us all in your debt. I confess I am
appalled at the casuistry of the majority opinion." [3]

The Case

Fred Toyosoburo Korematsu was born of Japanese parents in
Oakland, California, in 1919. His early life was quite similar to
that of most people of his generation. He lived quietly with his
parents and three brothers in Oakland. Often he helped his father
who was a nurseryman. Most of his friends were Caucasians. In
fact, after graduation from Oakland High School he had fallen

---

[1] Eugene Gressman, "Mr. Justice Murphy—A Preliminary Appraisal,"
Columbia Law Review, L (January, 1950), 47.

[2] Howard J. Woodford, Jr., *Abstract of Thesis, op. cit.,* p. 412.

[3] Quoted in Eugene Gressman, "The Controversial Image of Mr. Justice
Murphy," *op. cit.,* n. 23, p. 639.

in love with a Caucasian girl. For a short while Fred attended a junior college but left because of little interest in the course offerings. Prior to Pearl Harbor he was rejected for the draft because of a minor physical deficiency. As a result, he enrolled in a course in welding to prepare for war work and took a job in a shipyard. After Pearl Harbor, he tried to enlist in the Army but was again rejected. He lost his job in the shipyard but before long was working in a steel fabricating plant.

The war was soon to have a drastic effect on Fred Korematsu's activities. At the time of Pearl Harbor he was one of about 112,000 persons of Japanese descent living on the west coast. Seventy thousand of these were American citizens. As Japan swept from victory to victory in the Pacific many began to fear an invasion of the west coast. Though there was not one instance of espionage or sabotage by any Japanese-American, a clamor soon arose for the exclusion of all persons of Japanese lineage from the coastal areas. Lieutenant General John L. De Witt, the military commander on the west coast, insisted that the evacuation of all Japanese-Americans—aliens and citizens alike—was essential to the military defense of the area. Secretary of War Henry L. Stimson was reluctant to remove the Japanese from the west coast because he believed that De Witt exaggerated the situation and because he felt that such a removal would "make a tremendous hole in our constitutional system." However, as the pressure for evacuation from De Witt and others increased, Stimson reluctantly approved the exclusion plan.

It is now clear that military necessity alone was not responsible for the exclusion orders. Behind the plea of military necessity lay powerful anti-Japanese pressure groups, vocalized principally by the Hearst press. General De Witt himself later made his personal feelings known before a committee of the House of Representatives. He observed, "A Jap's a Jap and it makes no difference whether he is an American citizen or not. . . . I don't want any of them. We got them out. They were a dangerous element. The

West Coast is too vital and too vulnerable to take chances. . . .
You can't change [a Japanese] by giving him a piece of paper."

In February, 1942, President Franklin D. Roosevelt issued an
executive order authorizing Stimson or subordinate military com-
manders to establish military areas "from which any or all persons may be excluded." The next month Congress, by voice vote,
passed a law ratifying Roosevelt's executive order and sanction-
ing future limitations upon the Japanese on the west coast.
Penalities of up to $5,000 in fines and a year in prison were pro-
vided by Congress for violation of the executive order. Acting
under this blanket authority, De Witt first imposed a curfew on
all aliens and persons of Japanese ancestry which required them
to be in their homes from 8 P.M. to 6 A.M. Shortly thereafter, he
began to issue a number of exclusion orders transferring all
Japanese-Americans from parts of California, Oregon, Washington, and Arizona to relocation centers inland set up by the newly
created War Relocation Authority.

Fred Korematsu, like the other 7,927 Japanese-Americans from
Oakland, was ordered to report to an assembly center six miles
away for eventual transfer to a relocation center. Anxious to remain near his California girl friend, Korematsu refused to obey
the exclusion order. Instead he left town. He moved into a quiet
rooming house, got a job in a trailer park and tried to pass himself off as a Chinese. The ruse failed. He was picked up by two
military policemen, taken to jail, charged with violating the exclusion order and placed in military custody. Though ably defended by the San Francisco office of the American Civil Liberties Union, Korematsu was found guilty of knowingly violating
the exclusion order by a Federal District Court and placed
on probation for five years. A circuit court of appeals affirmed the
decision and Korematsu was sent to a relocation center in Topaz,
Utah. In 1944 his case finally came to the Supreme Court.

In 1943, in the case of *Hirabayashi* v. *United States,* the Supreme Court had unanimously upheld De Witt's curfew as a

proper wartime measure, without considering the other features
of the program. But Justice Murphy had gone along reluctantly
in the Hirabayashi case. In a concurring opinion he publicly proclaimed his uneasy apprehension in upholding the curfew order.
"Today is the first time, so far as I am aware," he said,

That we have sustained a substantial restriction of the personal liberty of citizens of the United States based upon the accident of race
or ancestry. Under the curfew order here challenged no less than
70,000 American citizens have been placed under a special ban and
deprived of their liberty because of their particular racial inheritance.
In this sense it bears a melancholy resemblance to the treatment
accorded to members of the Jewish race in Germany and other parts
of Europe. The result is the creation in this country of two classes of
citizens for the purposes of a critical and perilous hour—to sanction
discrimination between groups of United States citizens on the basis
of ancestry. In my opinion, this goes to the very brink of constitutional
power.

Given such doubts it seemed clear that Murphy would not
approve the more drastic exclusion program. But what about the
rest of the Court? Could Murphy count on the support of liberal
justices such as Black, Douglas, and Rutledge? On December 18,
1944, just as the relocation centers were about to be dismantled,
the Supreme Court handed down its decision in *Korematsu v.
United States*. It was a surprising line-up indeed! Justice Black
wrote the majority opinion sustaining De Witt's exclusion order
and thereby upheld Korematsu's conviction. He was joined by
Chief Justice Stone and Justices Reed, Douglas, and Rutledge.
Justice Frankfurter wrote a brief concurring opinion. Dissenting
opinions were written by Justices Jackson, Roberts, and Murphy.
The most vigorous, penetrating, and impassioned of the dissenting opinions by far was the one written by Justice Murphy which
indeed "went to the heart of the matter."

Justice Black's majority opinion was based largely on the argument that the Court could do nothing but accept the judgment of
the military in time of war. Relying heavily on the Hirabayashi

case Black reasoned that it was not beyond the war power of Congress and the President to direct the military to exclude those of Japanese ancestry from the coastal areas. "It is true," said Black,

that exclusion from the area in which one's home is located is a far greater deprivation than constant confinement to the home from 8:00 P.M. to 6:00 A.M. Nothing short of apprehension by the proper military authorities of the gravest imminent danger to the public safety can constitutionally justify either. But exclusion from a threatened area, no less than curfew, has a definite and close relationship to the prevention of espionage and sabotage. The military authorities, charged with the primary responsibility of defending our shores, concluded that curfew provided inadequate protection and ordered exclusion . . . Korematsu was not excluded from the military area because of hostility to him or his race. He *was* excluded because we are at war with the Japanese Empire, because the properly constituted military authorities feared an invasion of our West Coast and felt constrained to take proper security measures, because they decided that the military urgency of the situation demanded that all citizens of Japanese ancestry be segregated from the West Coast temporarily, and finally, because Congress, reposing its confidence in this time of war in our military leaders—as inevitably it must—determined that they should have the power to do just this. There was evidence of disloyalty on the part of some, the military authorities considered that the need for action was great, and time was short. We cannot—by availing ourselves of the calm perspective of hindsight—now say that at the time these actions were unjustified.

Justice Murphy saw little merit in the majority argument of his good friend and erstwhile leader. He began his dissent by stating bluntly that the exclusion of Japanese-Americans from the Pacific coast area should not be approved. "Such exclusion," said Murphy, "goes over 'the very brink of constitutional power' and falls into the ugly abyss of racism." Although conceding that the war situation in 1942 was so grave that the judgments of military authorities were to be thoroughly respected, he painstakingly tried to show that the military demand for exclusion was completely unjustified in fact. Murphy argued that "the judicial test of whether the Government, on a plea of military necessity, can validly deprive an individual of any of his constitutional rights is whether the deprivation is reasonably related to a public danger that is so 'immediate, imminent, and impending' as not to admit of delay and not to permit the intervention of ordinary constitutional processes to alleviate the danger." The exclusion order banishing Korematsu from his home did not meet that test. Instead, the order was "an obvious racial discrimination" which deprived Korematsu and others of their rights under the Fifth Amendment. It further deprived them of their rights "to live and work where they will, to establish a home where they choose and to move about freely. In excommunicating them without benefit of hearings, this order also deprives them of all their constitutional rights to procedural due process."

Murphy cited a number of statements and remarks made by General De Witt to show that his demands for exclusion were based on racial rather than military considerations. For example, De Witt had condemned *all* individuals of Japanese descent as "subversives" who should be "wiped off the map." He referred to the Japanese as "an enemy race" whose "racial strains are undiluted." Murphy thus argued that De Witt justified exclusion by relying upon "questionable racial and sociological" principles which are not "ordinarily within the realm of expert military judgment." In short, all the reasons advanced for exclusion stem from an "accumulation of much of the misinformation, half-truths and insinuations that for years have been directed against Japanese-Americans by people with racial and economic prejudices—the same people who have been among the foremost advocates of evacuation." A military judgment based upon such considerations which have been largely discredited by experts "is not entitled to the great weight ordinarily given the judgments based on strictly military considerations."

Murphy was quick to admit that the coastal areas contained some disloyal persons of Japanese descent.

But to infer that examples of individual disloyalty prove group disloyalty and justify discriminatory action against the entire group is to deny that under our system of law individual guilt is the sole basis for deprivation of rights. Moreover, this inference, which is at the very heart of the evacuation orders, has been used in support of the abhorrent and despicable treatment of minority groups by the dictatorial tyrannies which this nation is now pledged to destroy. To give constitutional sanction to that inference in this case, however well-intentioned may have been the military command on the Pacific Coast, is to adopt one of the cruelest of the rationales used by our enemies to destroy the dignity of the individual and to encourage and open the door to discriminatory actions against other minority groups in the passions of tomorrow.

To Murphy, mass exclusion could not be justified since there had been sufficient time to hold individual loyalty hearings. The first exclusion order was not issued until four months after Pearl Harbor, and the evacuation was not completed until eleven months later. Moreover, during a period of six months the British had set up hearing boards to examine over 70,000 aliens on an individual basis. Even in the United States the loyalty of persons of German and Italian ancestry had been determined on an individual basis. Hence, "it seems incredible," said Murphy, "that under these circumstances it would have been impossible to hold loyalty hearings for the mere 112,000 persons involved—or at least for the 70,000 American citizens—especially when a large part of this number represented children and elderly men and women. Any inconvenience that may have accompanied an attempt to conform to procedural due process cannot be said to justify violations of constitutional rights of individuals."

In the final paragraph of his dissenting opinion which, according to one writer, "should be engraved in stone," Murphy's passionate commitment to individual freedom for all men is eloquently revealed. "I dissent," said Murphy,

from this legalization of racism. Racial discrimination in any form and in any degree has no justifiable part whatever in our democratic way of life. It is unattractive in any setting but it is utterly revolting among a free people who have embraced the principles set forth in the Constitution of the United States. All residents of this nation are kin in some way by blood or culture to a foreign land. Yet they are primarily and necessarily a part of the new and distinct civilization of the United States. They must accordingly be treated at all times as the heirs of the American experiment and as entitled to all the rights and freedoms guaranteed by the Constitution.

Obviously troubled by the Korematsu decision, the Supreme Court, on the same day, held in *Ex Parte Endo* that a Japanese-American girl of proven loyalty could not be held in a war relocation center. Speaking through Justice Douglas, a unanimous Court reasoned simply that neither Congress nor the President had empowered the War Relocation Authority to *continue* the detention of Japanese-Americans once their loyalty had been established. Nevertheless, the Court's evasion of the major constitutional issues and refusal to invalidate the entire internment program evoked a sharp concurring opinion from Justice Murphy. "I join in the opinion of the Court," said Murphy, "but I am of the view that detention in Relocation Centers of persons of Japanese ancestry regardless of loyalty is not only unauthorized by Congress or the Executive but is another example of the unconstitutional resort to racism inherent in the entire evacuation program. As stated more fully in my dissenting opinion in *Korematsu* v. *United States,* . . . racial discrimination of this nature bears no reasonable relation to military necessity and is utterly foreign to the ideals and traditions of the American people."

THE "CALM PERSPECTIVE OF HINDSIGHT"

In the "calm perspective of hindsight" we have reason to be grateful for Murphy's impassioned Korematsu dissent. There is now no doubt that the compulsory evacuation of Japanese-Americans from the west coast was the most flagrant and shocking denial of constitutional rights in American history. For stripped of the niceties of language, what the Army did was to take 70,000 American citizens and 52,000 aliens, most of whom were ineligible for citizenship by law, and lock them up in virtual concentration camps for the duration of the war without ever charging them with any crime! No wonder then that the entire exclusion program has been almost universally condemned by responsible commentators as "an evil blotch on our national history."

In what is probably the most complete study of the evacuation program, three authors have drawn conclusions that are reminiscent of Murphy's dissenting opinion. Noting that the plea of military necessity could not be sustained, they point out that the exclusion program "violated and degraded the basic individualism which sustains a democracy. It impaired the trial tradition of the common law. It disparaged the principle that guilt is individual. It sapped the vitality of the precept of equality. It made racism a constitutional principle. It tolerated preventive incarceration for assumed disloyal beliefs and attitudes—unaccompanied by acts—attributing them without proof, probable cause, or reasonable suspicion to an entire group on a basis of race. Recklessly and unnecessarily, it loosened judicial control of the military and produced dangerous imbalance in our government." [1] Deploring the failure of the Supreme Court to uphold individual rights, the authors argue that "if the Court had struck down the program, the Japanese American episode would have lived in history as nothing more than a military blunder." [2] In approving the program the Court "abandoned the Constitution to military fiat" and thereby jeopardized the liberty of all Americans.

Many others have reached similar conclusions. One careful

[1] Jacobus ten Broek; Edward N. Barnhart; Floyd W. Matson; *Prejudice, War and the Constitution* (Berkeley and Los Angeles: University of California Press, 1954), p. 325.
[2] *Ibid.*, 332.

student remarked in 1949 that the exclusion process "betrayed all Americans," and that Black's Korematsu opinion could not be justified. The decision was "a too-easy acquiescence" to the military. Only six months after the Korematsu opinion was handed down, a law school professor characterized our treatment of Japanese-Americans as "hasty, unnecessary and mistaken." He concluded that the Korematsu decision ignored "the rights of citizenship, and the safeguards of trial practice which have been the historical attributes of liberty. Beyond that, it is an injustice, and therefore, like the trials of Sacco, Vanzetti, and Dreyfus, a threat to society, and to all men. We believe that the German people bear a common political responsibility for outrages secretly committed by the Gestapo and the S.S. What are we to think of our own part in a program which violates every democratic social value, yet has been approved by the Congress, the President, and the Supreme Court?" [1]

Under the circumstances, should not Justice Murphy's dissent find a place as one of democracy's great documents?

[1] Eugene V. Rostow, "The Japanese American Cases—A Disaster," *Yale Law Journal*, June, 1945, p. 533. This article is also reprinted in Rostow's *The Sovereign Prerogative: The Supreme Court and the Quest for Law* (New Haven: Yale University Press, 1962). Of particular interest is an *addendum* noting the measures taken to redress Japanese-Americans by the federal government for grievances suffered, pp. 263-266.

VIII

Justice Wiley B. Rutledge
and the Yamashita Case

Of how a warm, kindly Justice from the Middle West, who some said was a weakling on the Court, rose to the defense of a defeated, disgraced Japanese general sentenced to death for atrocities committed by his troops.

THE MAN

NOT EVEN A writer of fiction with the wildest conceivable imagination would have dared to dream that the paths of Wiley Blount Rutledge and Tomoyuki Yamashita would ever cross. For when Yamashita was already nine years of age and living in a country village near Hiroshima (which was later destined to suffer through the terrible holocaust of the world's first atomic bomb), Rutledge was just beginning life in Cloversport, Kentucky, as the son of a circuit-riding Baptist minister. Rutledge spent the first six years of his life from 1894 to 1900 in Cloversport and then moved with his family to Asheville, North Carolina. Three years later the family moved back to Kentucky for a short stay before settling down near Maryville in eastern Tennessee. Rutledge thus grew up in the mountains of Tennessee "among people who drew no distinctions except between folks and foreigners. He accepted the standards with one modification

This chapter appeared as an article in *Social Science*, XXXVII, No. 3 (June, 1962). Reprinted by permission.

—there were no foreigners."[1] Rutledge attended Maryville College, a small Presbyterian school, where he majored in classics. One of his teachers of Greek at the college was Annabel Person of Howell, Michigan. Rutledge later married her in 1917. In the meantime, he decided to study chemistry and transferred to the University of Wisconsin, where he received his Bachelor of Arts degree in 1914.

Shortly after graduation from Wisconsin, Rutledge decided he was interested in law rather than chemistry. But since there was no money to finance a legal education, he began to teach in high school while concurrently studying law at Indiana University. The double strain of teaching and study broke his health. Rutledge contracted tuberculosis and was forced to return to Ashville for a year's rest before returning to work as secretary to the Board of Education at Alburquerque, New Mexico. Two years later, in 1920, he moved to Boulder, Colorado where he again taught in the public schools while attending law classes at the University of Colorado. He finally obtained his law degree and began to practice law with a firm in Boulder. But in 1924 he returned to the University as a teacher in the law school. Rutledge remained on the Colorado campus until 1926, when he became a law professor at Washington University in St. Louis. He later served as dean of the law schools of Washington University and the University of Iowa. As teacher and dean, Rutledge was noted for his sincere and considerate interest in students. During this period Rutledge was fairly well known in law school circles even though he had not acquired a national reputation and was little known among lay citizens. He never sought or held any political office, but as a Democrat he was a stanch supporter of President Roosevelt and the New Deal. In a predominantly Republican area he spoke out openly in favor of the New Deal legislation and strongly criticized those Supreme Court decisions which nullified key measures of the Roosevelt administration.

[1] Irving Brant, "Mr. Justice Rutledge—the Man," *Iowa Law Review* XXXV (Summer, 1950), 546.

In April, 1939, President Roosevelt appointed Rutledge to the United States Court of Appeals for the District of Columbia. On that court Rutledge made a reputation as a sound, fair and politically liberal judge. In 1943 President Roosevelt made his eighth and last appointment to the Supreme Court when he elevated Rutledge to the post of associate justice. Rutledge was the least known of Roosevelt's appointees, but he had the support of many conservatives as well as liberals for the post. The conservative Democratic senator from Iowa, Guy M. Gillette, for example, had long been urging Rutledge's appointment to the Court. In addition, Rutledge's appointment was influenced by the fact that he "had geography"—that is he was a midwestern who was needed on the Court to keep the sectional balance which Presidents normally try to maintain.

Justice Rutledge was a stocky, rugged, and determined man who had an unbridled faith in democratic institutions. The late Harold Ickes once said of him that he "believed in the essential dignity of human life, the encroachment upon which, even as to a single individual, would be an affront to the natural and proper pride of the group. He was so deeply imbued with democracy, his whole being was so permeated by its spirit, that it was reflected from him as candlelight from a mirror." [1] He had an unlimited capacity for friendship with people everywhere and in every walk of life. He was a close friend of grocers, taxicab drivers, law clerks, Supreme Court building guards, and famous lawyers and cabinet officials as well. He genuinely loved people—all people.

This was no theoretical or abstract philosophical concept to him; it was a matter of daily living. During the years of his development in the midwest, Wiley Rutledge learned well the beliefs, hopes, fears, thoughts, emotions, and labors of people of all walks of life. He constantly and frequently sought the company of other people. . . . He sought associations with all kinds of people whose life stories and

[1] I. H. Ickes, "Justice Rutledge," *New Republic*, September 26, 1949, p. 20.

opinions he liked to hear informally. Wiley Rutledge wanted to know
what others were thinking, what they believed. He was a man of
merry heart and cheerful countenance. He had the faculty of gener-
ating sincere discussion without himself dominating the group. He
listened well and he understood. Having understanding, he had wisdom.[1]

Such was the man whom the American West had sent forth to
the Supreme Court. Rutledge brought with him to the Court all
his fine qualities of compassion and independent liberalism. He
gave himself completely to the Court's work, writing his opinions
slowly and with great care, not because of personal ambition but
because of his desire to promote the general good in each decision he wrote. Although he was responsible for important decisions in areas such as interstate commerce and taxation, Justice
Rutledge will always be best remembered for his opinions in
behalf of American individual liberties. In case after case his
passion for justice is fully revealed in bold, straightforward
language.

Along with his colleague, Justice Murphy, he believed firmly
that the Supreme Court's most vital responsibility in an era of extensive governmental power was the protection of personal liberty. Government intrusions into the private rights and privileges
of individuals simply could not be tolerated if democracy was to
survive. This faith was expressed best in his own words in the
introduction to his small book written in 1947 entitled *Declaration of Legal Faith*. "I believe in law," he said. "At the same time
I believe in freedom. And I know that each of these things may
destroy the other. But I know too, that, without both, neither can
long endure . . . justice too is a part of life, of evolution, of man's
spiritual growth. . . . Law, freedom, and justice—this trinity is the
object of my faith."

[1] Proceedings in Memory of Justice Rutledge before U. S. Supreme Court,
reproduced in *Iowa Law Review*, XXXVI (Summer, 1951), 593. Reprinted
by permission.

Justice Rutledge's life was "devoted to an attempt to effect an accommodation between freedom and law, to conjoin freedom and justice with law." [1] Nowhere is this better demonstrated than in his dissenting opinion in the case of Tomoyuki Yamashita.

THE CASE

While Wiley Rutledge was carving out a career as teacher, lawyer, and judge, Tomoyuki Yamashita had already been well prepared, quite by accident, for a military career. Yamashita was the son of a country doctor but, unlike his older brother, he did not follow his father's profession. Once asked why he had chosen the life of a professional soldier Yamashita remarked, "It was perhaps my destiny. I did not choose this career. My father suggested the idea because I was big and healthy and my mother did not seriously object, bless her soul, as she thought that I would never pass the highly competitive entrance examination. I went to Hiroshima, took the competitive examination, passed it and found myself headed for the Cadets' Academy." [2]

In 1908 Yamashita was commissioned a second lieutenant of infantry in the Japanese Army. He rose slowly but surely through the ranks, serving on various assignments with the Japanese general staff and as a military attache in Austria for a short period of time. During these years he earned a reputation as an industrious, gentle, kindhearted and fairminded officer who wanted the Japanese Army to be developed and used principally for defense purposes. By 1936 Yamashita was a major general with an infantry brigade in Korea. He subsequently served in North China and Manchuria and as inspector general of the air service in Tokyo. But Yamashita never received the best military assign-

[1] *Ibid*, p. 606.
[2] A. Frank Reel, *The Case of General Yamashita* (Chicago: University of Chicago Press, 1949), pp. 58-59. Reprinted by permission.

ments, largely because he had irritated the powerful War Minister, General Tojo, and his military clique. This entrenched
military group resented Yamashita's less warlike tendencies.

When the Japanese bombed Pearl Harbor on December 7,
1941, Yamashita was put in charge of the Malayan campaign. In
February, 1942, Yamashita became a national hero when he concluded the campaign with the astounding capture of Singapore
by numerically inferior Japanese troops. Outnumbered three to
one, the Japanese were able to surprise the British by moving
swiftly and unexpectedly down the Malaya peninsula toward
supposedly impregnable Singapore, which surrendered without
a fight. Overnight Yamashita became known as the ferocious,
brilliant conqueror—the "Tiger of Malaya." Yet Yamashita never
felt that the conquest of Singapore was particularly brilliant. To
him it was simply a "bluff that worked."

Despite this great victory Yamashita still was not looked upon
with favor by Tojo and his military clique. The new popular hero
was not even permitted to go home to receive the plaudits of a
grateful people. Instead, he quickly found himself relegated to
an unimportant command in Manchukuo. In 1944 when the Tojo
cabinet fell and when the American occupation of the Philippines
appeared imminent, Yamashita was suddenly ordered from Manchukuo to relieve the inept Commander of the Japanese troops
in the islands. After spending only four days in Tokyo, he arrived
in Manila on October 7, 1944. Just nine days later American
troops invaded Leyte, and Yamashita withdrew to the mountains
of Northern Luzon leaving only a small detachment of soldiers
in the city. After the withdrawal, Manila and the rest of the
Philippines suffered through one of the most unbelievable orgies
of mass murder, rape, and pillage ever recorded in the annals of
war. On September 3, 1945, General Yamashita came down the
mountains of Northern Luzon and surrendered the remnants of
his army and his seven-hundred-year-old samurai sword to an
American major general. He was immediately imprisoned in

Manila and was charged with being a war criminal. The charge read as follows:

Tomoyuki Yamashita, General Imperial Japanese Army, between 9, October, 1944 and 2, September, 1945, at Manila and at other places in the Philippine Islands, while commander of armed forces of Japan at war with the United States of America and its allies, unlawfully disregarded and failed to discharge his duty as commander to control the operations of the members of his command, permitting them to commit brutal atrocities and other high crimes against the people of the United States and of its allies and dependencies, particularly the Philippines; and he, General Tomoyuki Yamashita, thereby violated the laws of war.[1]

An American military commission of three major generals and two brigadier generals was named to try General Yamashita. Rules for the conduct of the trial were issued in a letter by General Douglas MacArthur who commanded the American forces in the Pacific. The letter virtually rescinded the ordinary rules of evidence since it allowed rumors, hearsay, and opinion to be used against General Yamashita. Not one of the members of the military commission was a lawyer. Six American officers were named to prosecute the case while six others were appointed to defend the defeated general. On October 8, 1945, Yamashita was arraigned before the commission and pleaded not guilty. At the arraignment, the defense was presented with a bill of particulars setting forth in detail sixty-four crimes committed by troops under Yamashita's command. Three weeks later a supplemental bill charging him with fifty-nine more crimes was filed. A defense motion for a continuance to study the new charges was denied by the commission. On the same day, October 29, 1945, the trial began in the shell-scarred ballroom of the American High Commissioner's residence in Manila before some three hundred eager spectators.

[1] *Ibid.,* p. 32.

As the trial opened, General Yamashita, who was said to appear "tame, safe and froglike" in his green uniform, sat quietly at a long table. The prosecution proceeded to present evidence designed to prove that Yamashita had failed to discharge his duties as a Commander by permitting his troops to commit atrocities against civilians and prisoners of war. Some 270 witnesses were called to the stand. In addition, photographs and affidavits secured by army investigators were introduced as evidence. One needed a strong stomach indeed not to be completely revolted by the recital of atrocities. Witness after witness described mass killings, bayoneting, defiling of bodies, mutilation, and mass raping of girls under twelve years of age. The horror involved in the brutal killing of over 30,000 people in this unleashed madness cannot be imagined without the recital of one or two specific items from the trial record.[1]

On March 21, 1945, two captured American fliers were taken to a foxhole by several Japanese officers and soldiers. With their hands tied behind their backs, the Americans were forced to a kneeling position in the foxhole and struck on the back of the neck with a large sword. One of the Japanese officers then fired three shots into the body of one. Later, the other flier succeeded in getting out of the foxhole and asked for a drink of water. Instead, he was forced back into the foxhole which was covered with wood and saturated with gasoline. A Japanese soldier then set fire to the wood and the group watched the American burn to death.

A Chinese mother testified that Japanese soldiers dragged her two children from her and killed them with bayonets. She stated that she saw her young daughter "bayoneted right on the breast, which penetrated through the back. After I saw that my children were wounded I was bayoneted on my back five times."

[1] Much of what follows is taken from the *Trial Record* noted in the bibliography. Also helpful was an interview with A. Frank Reel in New York City on March 22, 1961.

Such testimony made it difficult indeed to defend Yamashita. The general attitude toward the defendant in the courtroom is revealed well by the outburst of another Chinese woman from the witness stand who had seen her baby bayoneted by Japanese soldiers. She stared coldly at Yamashita and cried: "That Jap is to blame. He's got to be killed to pay for what he's done."

Despite the almost insurmountable difficulties faced by the defense, Yamashita's laywers worked untiringly for his acquittal. They argued that Yamashita could not be held responsible for the atrocities because he had never ordered or condoned them. In fact, he had never known of them. Yamashita himself testified that upon his arrival in the Phillipines he had been completely involved in trying to organize his army so that the attack by superior American forces could be blunted. But although he remained in technical command, Yamashita had, in reality, lost control of his troops. Yamashita's lawyers emphasized the vagueness of the charges against him and argued that hearsay, gossip, rumor and opinion could not be admitted as evidence against their client. The defense argued also that there was not sufficient time to prepare the case and objected to the severe limitations placed on cross-examination. Thus the defense lawyers contended that General Yamashita was deprived of a fair trial in violation of the due process clause of the Fifth Amendment. In addition, they maintained that the prosecution had made no effort to charge or prove that Yamashita had violated the laws of war.

On December 7, 1945—the fourth anniversary of Pearl Harbor —the military commission, after urgings by General MacArthur that it would be fitting and appropriate to hand down a verdict on that day, found Yamashita guilty and sentenced him to death by hanging.

The majority of newspaper reporters at the trial felt that Yamashita had not been given a fair trial. Typical of the comments was this estimate of the trial cabled by a *Newsweek* correspondent.

In the opinion of probably every correspondent covering the trial, the military commission came into the courtroom the first day with the decision already in its collective pocket. The trial has not been particularly impressive, either from a legal standpoint or that of courtroom conduct. There is at least one uninhibited and constant doodler on the commission and another member who spends a large part of his time staring out the window. It is probably true that Yamashita actually is 'legally' guilty according to the 'extra-legal' principle of command responsibility. But as one correspondent put it: It's like a man being tried rightly or wrongly for rape, and finding the girl's father is the judge.[1]

Convinced of his innocence, Yamashita's defense lawyers worked feverishly to obtain a review of the case. General MacArthur, as expected, refused to grant clemency. The Supreme Court of the Philippines refused to hear the case. But on December 20, 1945, the Supreme Court of the United States met in special session and agreed to hear the case. On January 7, 1946, oral argument began before the Court, with three of General Yamashita's original defense lawyers who had been flown to Washington appearing in behalf of their client. On Monday, February 4, 1946 the Court handed down its decision in an opinion read by Chief Justice Stone which has been described as a "patchwork of ideas and statements, pieced together to satisfy the divergent views of men who were seeking to find 'good' reasons for a politically expedient result." [2] In brief, the Court ruled that the trial of General Yamashita by the military commission was lawful. The General could be executed. Stone argued that the Court was not concerned with the guilt or innocence of General Yamashita, but only with whether or not the military commission had been lawfully created to try him for the offense charged. Since Congress had the authority to create military commissions for the trial of enemy combatants whose proceedings were not reviewable by the Courts, there was no reason to inter-

[1] Robert Shaplen, *Newsweek*, December 10, 1945, p. 44.
[2] A. Frank Reel, *op. cit.*, p. 216.

fere with the trial. The Court sidestepped the crucial issue of a fair trial under the Fifth Amendment by stating that the rulings of the military commission on the evidence and the mode of conducting trials are reviewable *only* by higher military authorities.

Chief Justice Stone was joined in his opinion by Justices Black, Burton, Douglas, Frankfurter, and Reed. Justice Jackson took no part in the case since he was then in Germany as chief prosecutor for the United States in the Nuremberg trials. Justices Murphy and Rutledge dissented sharply. In fact they read their dissenting opinions "in tones so bitter and in language so sharp that it was readily apparent to all listeners that even more acrimonious expression must have marked the debate behind the scenes."[1] As soon as the Chief Justice had read the Court's opinion, Justice Murphy presented his dissent in a voice "ringing with indignation."

Murphy, who as Governor General of the Philippines before his appointment to the Court had acquired a great love of the island people, was concerned principally with the great issue of a fair trial, which issue the majority opinion had refused to face. To Murphy the answer was plain. Since the due process clause of the Fifth Amendment guarantees procedural rights to "any person" accused of a crime by the federal government, Yamashita was protected by the Constitution. Murphy noted that "the failure of the military commission to obey the dictates of the due process requirements of the Fifth Amendment are apparent in this case. . . . No military necessity or other emergency demanded the suspension of the safeguards of due process." Yet Yamashita

was rushed to trial under an improper charge, given insufficient time to prepare an adequate defense, deprived of the benefits of some of the most elementary rules of evidence and summarily sentenced to be hanged. In all this needless and unseemly haste there was no serious attempt to charge or to prove that he committed a recognized violation of the laws of war. He was not charged with personally participating in the acts of atrocity or with ordering or condoning their commission.

[1] *Ibid.*

Not even knowledge of these crimes was attributed to him. It was simply alleged that he unlawfully disregarded and failed to discharge his duty as commander to control the operations of the members of his command, permitting them to commit the acts of atrocity. The recorded annals of warfare and the established principles of international law afford not the slightest precedent for such a charge. This indictment in effect permitted the military commission to make the crime whatever it willed, dependent upon its biased view as to petitioner's duties and his disregard thereof, a practice reminiscent of that pursued in certain less respected nations in recent years.

Murphy prophesied that "in the sober afterglow will come the realization of the boundless and dangerous implications of the procedure sanctioned today."

In an air obviously tense, Justice Rutledge rose to deliver his masterful dissenting opinion. He had worked hard to get a hearing for Yamashita and had succeeded by the narrowest of margins. He had worked night and day under pressure to write his long thirty-two page dissent. He began by noting that it was not easy to find "his views at odds with the Court's in a matter of this character and gravity. Only the most deeply felt convictions could force one to differ. That reason alone leads me to do so now, against strong considerations for withholding dissent." As he spoke the last phrase Rutledge "carefully turned and nodded in the chief justice's direction."

More is at stake than General Yamashita's fate. There could be no possible sympathy for him if he is guilty of the atrocities for which his death is sought. But there can be and should be justice administered according to law. In this stage of war's aftermath it is too early for Lincoln's great spirit, best lighted in the Second Inaugural, to have wide hold for the treatment of foes. It is not too early, it is never too early, for the Nation steadfastly to follow its great constitutional traditions, none older or more universally protective against unbridled power than due process of law in the trial and punishment of men, that is, of all men, whether citizens, aliens, alien enemies or enemy belligerents. It can become too late.

Rutledge used his strongest language in deploring the lack of a fair trial for Yamashita.

This trial is unprecedented in our history. Never before have we tried and convicted an enemy general for action taken during hostilities or otherwise in the course of military operations or duty. Much less have we condemned one for failing to take action. The novelty is not lessened by the trial's having taken place after hostilities ended and the enemy, including the accused, had surrendered. . . .

It is not in our tradition for anyone to be charged with crime which is defined after his conduct, alleged to be criminal, has taken place; or in language not sufficient to inform him of the nature of the offense or to enable him to make defense. . . .

It is outside our basic scheme to condemn men without giving reasonable opportunity for preparing defense; in capital or other serious crimes to convict on official documents, affidavits, documents or translations thereof, diaries, photographs, motion picture films, and newspapers or on hearsay, once, twice or thrice removed, more particularly when the documentary evidence or some of it is prepared *ex parte* by the prosecuting authority and includes not only opinion but conclusions of guilt. Nor in such cases do we deny the rights of confrontation of witnesses and cross-examination.

Rutledge discussed additional deviations from the fundamental law and concluded that Yamashita had been denied due process under the Fifth Amendment. Bit by bit Rutledge carefully dissected each of the other findings of the military commission. On the last page of his dissent he stated concisely his arguments against the majority opinion. "The difference," he said, "between the Court's view of this proceeding and my own comes down in the end to the view, on the one hand, that there is no law restrictive upon these proceedings other than whatever rules and regulations may be prescribed for their government by the executive authority or the military and, on the other hand, that the provisions of the Articles of War, of the Geneva Convention and the Fifth Amendment apply." Finally, Justice Rutledge remarked that he could not "accept the view that anywhere in our system resides or lurks a power so unrestrained to deal with any human being through any process of trial. What military agencies or authorities may do with our enemies in battle or invasion, apart from proceedings in the nature of trial and some semblance of judicial action, is beside the point. Nor has any human being heretofore been held to be wholly beyond elementary procedural protection by the Fifth Amendment. I cannot consent to even implied departure from that great absolute. It was a great patriot [Thomas Paine] who said: 'He that would make his own liberty secure must guard even his enemy from oppression; for if he violates this duty he establishes a precedent that will reach himself.' "

Along with Justice Murphy, Rutledge had fought hard for Yamashita but now, with the verdict in, he felt lost and alone. "I suppose I'll be crucified," he remarked after delivering his dissenting opinion. But to his great surprise, many people came to the support of his views. Letters praising his stand came from many Americans who quickly grasped the fact that the refusal "to compel a fair trial of a Japanese war Prisoner was not only shocking in itself but threatened the liberty of every American citizen." Nevertheless, Stone's majority opinion had won the day. Yamashita appeared doomed. Yet his dedicated defense lawyers continued to have some hope.

Before Yamashita could be executed, the sentence had to be approved by General MacArthur. The defense hoped that General MacArthur would be moved to grant clemency on the basis of the dissenting opinions. But shortly after being notified by radio that the Court had refused to issue a writ of habeas corpus in behalf of Yamashita and *before* seeing the photostatic copies of the decision, General MacArthur ordered that Yamashita be hanged in disgrace—"stripped of uniform, decorations, and other appurtenances signifying membership in the military profession." MacArthur's true sentiments were revealed clearly in the order, for at one point he stated that the proceedings of the military commission "were guided by that primary rationale of all judicial purpose—to ascertain the full truth *unshackled by any artificialities of narrow method or technical arbitrariness.* The results are beyond challenge." This statement makes it quite obvious that, in the famous words of Justice Brandeis, "the greatest dangers to liberty lurk in insidious encroachment by men of zeal, well-meaning, but without understanding."

MacArthur was taken to task for his statement only five days later by Justice Murphy in another dissenting opinion in which Justice Rutledge joined. Murphy pointed out, "All those who act by virtue of the authority of the United States are bound to respect the principles of justice codified in our Constitution. Those principles which were established after so many centuries of struggle, can scarcely be dismissed as *narrow artificialities* or *arbitrary technicalities.* They are the very life blood of our civilization."

Only one final recourse remained open for the defense: an appeal to President Truman as Commander-in-Chief of the Armed Forces for commutation of Yamashita's death penalty to life imprisonment. The plea was made, but on February 8, 1946, the President announced that he would take no action on the petition.

Now everyone had spoken—the military commission, the Philippine Supreme Court, the Supreme Court of the United States, General MacArthur, and President Truman. Only two Supreme court justices, a brilliant defense staff and a handful of powerless people had been willing to speak out on behalf of Yamashita. His time had run out. There was nothing left to do but hang him.

Humanity has become so ashamed of "legally" killing people that executions usually take place in the dead of night, in isolated places with very few witnesses present. If possible, everything must be done under the cover of darkness. When the deed is done, the body must be disposed of quickly before the next dawn lest the light of day reveal to others what has transpired. And so it was that on February 3, 1946, at three o'clock in the

morning, in an isolated Philippine cane field near Los Bоñas, a
town just thirty-five miles south of Manila, General Yamashita,
stripped of his uniform and dressed in ill-fitting G.I. fatigue
clothes, strode up the thirteen steps of a rudely constructed
scaffold. Only two minutes later, under the glare of three flood-
lights, the trap was sprung. Yamashita's neck was broken and he
died the dishonorable death of a convicted war criminal. His
body was cut down, sewn up in a blanket, and immediately
buried in an unmarked grave next to those of some of his soldiers.

"Sober Afterglow"

Yamashita died and no one mourned. MacArthur was avenged.
Less than four years after Yamashita's execution, Justice Rutledge
suffered a cerebral hemorrhage and died in York, Maine on September 10, 1949, at the age of fifty-five. He had served only six
years on the Court. But the issues of the Yamashita case live on.
It may be a long time before the full impact of Rutledge's dissent is felt. But "if the United States is still a free country a
hundred years from now, this dissenting opinion will be one of
the stoutest bases of its freedom." It was one of the truly great
justices—Justice Brandeis—who once said, "If we would guide by
the light of reason, we must let our minds be bold." No opinion
better illustrates Rutledge's commitment to that notion than his
Yamashita dissent.

But perhaps we are too idealistic. It may well be, as one writer
has suggested, that after a bitter war, it is necessary "to purge
our residual vindictiveness by killing captured foes." But if this
is so, it would have been better if Yamashita had been taken out
and hanged from the "nearest lamp-post rather than to have
sullied our American concepts of justice by a farcical trial." [1] For
it must be remembered that Yamashita was not tried by an international court. He was tried, convicted, and executed on Ameri-

[1] Newman Levy, Review of "The Case of General Yamashita," *The
Saturday Review*, October 8, 1949, p. 59.

can territory by Americans presumably operating under the rules of American criminal procedures. But as an example of American administration of justice his trial was indeed a grisly farce.

There can be little doubt that in the handling of this case "our Army missed a great opportunity. Having fought and won a war against totalitarianism . . . we could have shown the world just what we meant. Instead of that, we fell to the level of our enemies. We adopted their judicial techniques. We gave the world a practical demonstration of the fact that, certainly in one corner of the globe, 'the enemy has lost the battle but has destroyed our ideals.' " [1] Yet by the time of Justice Rutledge's death the military had not even begun to learn this lesson.

In 1949, A. Frank Reel, one of Yamashita's defense lawyers and former Army captain, published the book entitled, *The Case of General Yamashita,* which has been cited in this chapter. Reel argued vehemently that the Yamashita case had been wrongly decided. Among other things, he maintained that Yamashita had not had a fair trial and that America must acknowledge this mistake to the world. And what was the reaction of our military to this book? *They banned it!* After a Japanese newspaper printed a brief review of Reel's book, a major from General MacArthur's headquarters in then occupied Japan informed the editors of Tokyo papers that it would be "advisable" not to mention the book in the future. At the same time, a Tokyo publishing house was "cautioned" not to publish the book in the Japanese language. On November 22, 1949 a *Memorandum* was issued by Mac-Arthur's headquarters under the signature of Brigadier General Courtney Whitney stating the Army's objections to the book. Whitney stated categorically that the book was banned because American prestige, dignity, and security were at stake. He maintained that the book was designed

to arouse in the minds of the Japanese doubt as to the moral standards of the American people and to impugn the integrity of the judicial process leading to judgments rendered in the trials for war crimes.

[1] A. Frank Reel, *op. cit.,* p. 241.

The best that can be said for this effort to propagate among the Japanese people the false concept that Yamashita was denied the protection of elementary justice is that it is based upon a profit motive—the worst, that it is intended seriously to impair the American position in the Orient. Regardless, the end result would be the same. Passions of irresponsible elements would be aroused, minorities already in opposition would be strengthened, and American lives might well be forfeited. The better to insure that the book and the propaganda efforts of its publisher do not succeed in a perversion of the historical truth.[1]

This statement illustrates well the unfortunate cast of the military mind in such matters. It would appear that in the name of security almost any censorship can somehow be justified! Yet there is no evidence to indicate that there was serious opposition to the American occupation at that time nor that the distribution of Reel's book would strengthen what opposition there was. On the contrary, circulation of the book with the Army's blessing might well have heightened respect for American honesty and good faith. It is noteworthy that General Whitney saw fit to reproduce the entire majority opinion of the Supreme Court in the Appendix to his *Memorandum* but did not even mention, let alone reproduce, the Murphy and Rutledge dissents!

But if the military was so wrong in this case why did the Supreme Court refuse to grant jurisdiction in the first instance? The Court's majority opinion was based on the legally sound notion, well supported by previous cases, that the responsibility for the conduct of military trials was to be left to the executive branch of the Government. Justice Stone and others on the Court believed firmly that "Courts are not the only agency of government that must be assumed to have capacity to govern." Moreover, the Supreme Court has never shown great courage in protecting civil liberties during or immediately after a war. After all, war is carried on by the President and Congress, and for the Court

[1] "The Case of General Yamashita," *Memorandum*, General Hqs., Supreme Commander for the Allied Powers, Government Section, (November 22, 1949).

to inhibit their war-making powers might well be disastrous. Should not then the heavy moral responsibility for the conduct of military trials be left with the political arms of the government? Perhaps. Yet in the Yamashita case Chief Justice Stone missed a great opportunity for there was much at stake here. Without great difficulty and with real justification, the Court could easily have granted jurisdiction. Thus, it could have set an important precedent which would have served as a warning to military commissions to conduct their trials in accordance with the minimum requirements of fair procedure. By refusing to do so, the Court openly invited military courts to disregard our constitutional tradition. But perhaps, given the time and circumstances, it was too much to ask. "Perhaps Rutledge was fighting for the impossible in his Yamashita dissent. His fight was for the nation to rise to his ideals of democracy in the treatment of a defeated enemy. He fought the same fight for minority groups, for persons accused of crime—for all, without consideration of race, creed or color. 'The gap between his understanding and the nation's performance is the measure of stature to which he rose and of the distance we must travel if humanity is indeed to achieve its destiny.'" [1]

[1] Howard Mann, "Mr. Justice Rutledge and Civil Liberties," *Iowa Law Review*, XXXV (Summer, 1950), 681.

EPILOGUE

In an all-but-forgotten case, a white girl of eighteen was raped near a cemetery just outside Chattanooga, Tennessee, on the evening of January 22, 1906. Two days later a Negro, Ed Johnson, was arrested and charged with the crime. He was kept in a Nashville jail because passions were running high in his own community and it was feared he might be lynched. Throughout his brief three-day trial Johnson maintained his innocence. Witnesses were produced who testified that Johnson was working in a saloon about a mile away when the crime was committed. The girl could not positively identify Johnson as her assailant but testified that she "believed" Johnson was the man. On February 11, 1906, Johnson was convicted of rape and sentenced to death by hanging. March 13 was fixed as the date of execution.

Three local white lawyers assigned to defend Johnson agreed that no appeal should be taken because any delay in carrying out the execution might result in mob violence! However, two Negro attorneys, with the aid of funds collected by local Negro churches, filed a petition for habeas corpus on behalf of Johnson in a Federal Circuit Court on the ground that his constitutional rights had been violated. Specifically, they argued that all Negroes had been systematically excluded from the grand and petit juries of the county, and that Johnson's assigned lawyers were unable to defend him properly because of threatened mob violence.

On March 19 the Federal Circuit Court ruled that no federal question was involved and dismissed the appeal. However, the court ordered that Johnson be held for ten days so that he could appeal to the Supreme Court. This action forced the Governor to set another date for the execution. March 20 was the new date set.

In the meantime, Justice Harlan first heard the appeal and on March 19 the Supreme Court allowed the appeal and issued an order staying the execution, set for the next day. On the afternoon of March 19 the Court's order was telegraphed to Sheriff Joseph H. Shipp and his deputies who were holding Johnson in custody. That evening a full account of the Court's action was circulated in the papers of Chattanooga. Nevertheless, the usual guards protecting Johnson from possible mob violence were withdrawn from the jail. Only one night jailer was left on duty.

At approximately 9 o'clock on the evening of March 19, a mob of about twenty men broke into the jail and battered down doors leading to Johnson's cell. While the mob was still in the jail, Sheriff Shipp arrived but he made no effort to protect Johnson. Still protesting his innocence, Johnson was dragged to a county bridge six blocks from the jail. He was hanged to the second span of the bridge with a trolley rope and his body was riddled with bullets. The Supreme Court's order had been effectively thwarted!

The Court was shocked by this open defiance of its mandate. Shortly after the lynching, however, Sheriff Shipp, who was running for re-election, stated in a newspaper interview that the Supreme Court "was responsible for this lynching. The people were willing to let the law take its course until it became known that the case would probably not be disposed of for four or five years by the Supreme Court of the United States. The people would not submit to this and I do not wonder at it." An angry Supreme Court subsequently found Shipp, one of his deputies, and four citizens who had participated in the lynching, guilty of contempt.

Chief Justice Melville W. Fuller concluded after a careful review of all the facts that "Shipp not only made the work of the
mob easy, but in effect aided and abetted it." Fuller stated that
it was "plain that what created this mob and led to this lynching
was the unwillingness of its members to submit to the delay required for the appeal. The intent to prevent that delay by defeating the hearing of the appeal necessarily follows from the defendants' acts, and, if the life of anyone in the custody of the law
is at the mercy of a mob, the administration of justice becomes a
mockery. When this court granted a stay of execution on Johnson's application it became its duty to protect him until his case
should be disposed of. And when its mandate, issued for his protection, was defied, punishment of those guilty of such attempt
must be awarded." Shipp was sentenced to serve ninety days in
the District of Columbia jail. It marked the first instance in the
history of the Court that a person had been punished for contempt of the Supreme Court by imprisonment.

Interest in Sheriff Shipp and the other five defendants continued
unabated. A large crowd gathered at the railroad station to cheer
the convicted men before their departure for Washington to serve
their sentences. Details of how the prisoners spent their days in
jail were avidly reported in newspapers throughout the country.
Petitions signed by over 5,000 persons requesting a pardon for
Shipp were sent to President Taft. After serving his sentence,
Shipp came home a hero. Ten thousand cheering citizens greeted
him on his return to Chattanooga. A series of banquets and re-
ceptions were held in his honor. He was praised by United States
senators and other public officials. Shortly after his return he
was re-elected sheriff by an overwhelming majority of votes.

The lesson of the Shipp case is an obvious one. It is simply
that the Supreme Court cannot safeguard individual freedoms
alone. As we have seen in the various chapters of this book, individual justices may make significant contributions to raising the
standards of our civilization. Yet there are serious limitations inherent in the judicial process. The Court can do little or nothing

to enforce its decisions. It has neither the power of the purse nor of the sword. It has no committed pressure group, no devoted clientele. It cannot save a people from ruin. In the long run it must rely on the good will and faith of an informed and conscientious people who are deeply committed to constitutional government. For, as Learned Hand once so well said, "Liberty lies in the hearts of men and women; when it dies there, no constitution, no law, no court can save it."

REFERENCES

NOTES FOR CHAPTER 1

The Man

Though very few Taney letters and papers have been preserved, the Chief Justice has been the subject of a great number of books and articles. The Manuscript Division, Library of Congress, contains only a very few Taney items. The most important of these is a barely legible account in Taney's own handwriting of the struggle within the Jackson cabinet over the Bank of the United States. A few items relating to Taney are found in the Benjamin R. Curtis papers also in the Manuscript Division, Lirary of Congress, but these relate principally to the differences between the two justices over the Dred Scott case. An invaluable source for anyone studying Taney's career is TYLER, SAMUEL. *Memoir of Roger Brooke Taney.* Baltimore: John Murphy, 1872. Taney himself had asked Tyler, a personal friend, to write the book which contains the Chief Justice's unfinished account of his life and a number of personal letters. The chief weakness of

Tyler's book is that it makes no attempt whatsoever to be objective. In fact, Tyler states in the *preface* that the book is designed to "vindicate one who had been so misrepresented."

Probably the most thoroughly done and objective work on Taney is SWISHER, CARL B. *Roger B. Taney*. New York: Macmillan, 1935. Most useful is a lengthy bibliography, including manuscript collections, of materials available on Taney. A shorter treatment of Taney by the same author is found in *Mr. Justice*, ed. A. DUNHAM and P. B. KURLAND. Chicago: University of Chicago Press, 1956, pp. 203-229.

The following books are also extremely useful.

PALMER, BENJAMIN W. *Marshall and Taney: Statesmen of the Law*. Minneapolis: University of Minnesota Press, 1939.

SMITH, CHARLES W. *Roger B. Taney: Jacksonian Jurist*. Chapel Hill: University of North Carolina Press, 1936.

STEINER, BERNARD C. *Life of Roger Brooke Taney*. Baltimore: Williams and Wilkins, 1922.

A brief sketch of Taney's life and work is found in 2 Wall. IX-XII (1864). Brief accounts are also found in the following:

BATES, ERNEST S. *The Story of the Supreme Court*. Indianapolis and New York: Bobbs-Merrill, C. 5, 1936.

MIKELL, WILLIAM E. "Roger Brooke Taney," in LEWIS, WILLIAM D. *Great American Lawyers*. Philadelphia: John C. Winston, 1908, 77-194.

SILVER, DAVID M. *Lincoln's Supreme Court*. Urbana: University of Illinois Press, 1956.

UMBREIT, KENNETH B. *Our Eleven Chief Justices*. New York and London: Harpers, 1938. Taney is presented in pp. 197-246.

A most violent attack on Taney is contained in *The Unjust Judge: A Memorial of Roger Brooke Taney*. New York: Baker and Godwin, 1865.

The following articles were also utilized in preparing the chapter:

References

ARMSTRONG, WALTER P. "The Rehabilitation of Roger B. Taney," *Tennessee Law Review*, XIV (June, 1936), 205-218.

BEITZINGER, ALFONS J. "Chief Justice Taney and the Publication of Court Opinions," *Catholic University of America Law Review*, VII (January, 1958), 32-36.

COZART, A. W. "Marshall and Taney: A Parallel," *Georgia Law Review*, I, No. 2 (December, 1927), 33-37.

ELLIS, CHARLES M. "Roger Brooke Taney," *Atlantic Monthly*, XV (1865), 151-161.

HARRIS, ROBERT J. "Chief Justice Taney: Prophet of Reform and Reaction," *Vanderbilt Law Review*, X (February, 1957), 227-257.

JANONSEK, JOSEPH O. "Roger Brooke Taney: Man of Conscience," *Bar Association of District of Columbia Journal*, XII (June, 1945), 159-160.

MALLISON, ALBERT G. "The Political Theories of Roger B. Taney," *The Southwestern Political Science Quarterly*, I (1920), 219-240.

MENDELSON, WALLACE. "Chief Justice Taney—Jacksonian Judge," *University of Pittsburgh Law Review*, XII (Spring, 1951), 381-393.

RANSOM, WILLIAM L. "Roger Brooke Taney: Chief Justice of the Supreme Court of the United States, 1836-1864," *Georgetown Law Journal*, XXIV (May, 1936), 809-909.

RUSKOWSKI, C. W. "Catholics on the United States Supreme Court," *University of Detroit Law Journal*, XXXIV (April, 1952), 650-658.

WARREN, EARL. "Roger Brooke Taney: Fifth Chief Justice of the United States," *American Bar Association Journal*, XLI (June, 1955), 504-506.

The citation for the Dred Scott case is *Dred Scott v. Sanford*, 19 How. 393 (1857). Almost all of the references noted above discuss the case. For an exhaustive review see HOPKINS, VINCENT C. *Dred Scott's Case*. New York: Fordham University Press, 1951.

The Case

The citation for *Ex Parte Merryman* is 17 Fed. Cas. 9487 (1861). *Ex Parte Milligan* is cited as 4 Wall. 2 (1866). The Merryman case is discussed fully in many of the references noted above. The Swisher, Silver, and Steiner discussions of the case are most useful. A thorough analysis is also found in Fairman, Charles. *Mr. Justice Miller and the Supreme Court, 1862-1890.* Cambridge: Harvard University Press, 1939, pp. 69-78, and Haines, C. G. and Sherwood, F. H. *The Role of the Supreme Court in American Government and Politics, 1835-1864.* Berkeley and Los Angeles: University of California Press, 1957, pp. 454-466.

The Merryman case was widely discussed in the contemporary newspapers of the period. A number of accounts were read in the Newspaper Reference Room, Library of Congress. Most useful accounts are found in the following: *Baltimore American, Boston Atlas, New York Times, New York Tribune* and *Richmond Enquirer.*

Constitutional problems relating to the suspension of the writ of habeas corpus have been widely discussed. Two useful books are the following:

Fairman, Charles. *The Law of Martial Rule.* Chicago: Callaghan, 1930.

Randall, James S. *Constitutional Problems Under Lincoln.* Urbana: University of Illinois Press, 1951.

Other good discussions are found in the following articles:

Bowman, Harold M. "The Supreme Court's Part in Building the Nation." *Boston University Law Review,* XI, 445-484.

Fisher, Sidney G. "The Suspension of the Writ of Habeas Corpus during the War of the Rebellion," *Political Science Quarterly,*

III (1888), 454-488. A most useful list of pamphlets and papers published on the habeas corpus question during the Civil War is appended to Fisher's article.

PARKER, JOEL. "Habeas Corpus and Martial Law," *North American Review*, XCIII (1861), 471-518.

NOTES FOR CHAPTER 2

THE MAN

Most of the background material on Chief Justice Waite was developed from his private papers and letters, which were deposited in the Library of Congress by his grandson in 1958. For additional papers I am indebted to Mr. and Mrs. John Barker Waite of Ann Arbor, Michigan. They made available a Waite Genealogy, compiled by Mrs. Waite, and a number of old letters, clippings, and lithographs of the Waite family. The important letter written by Waite upon his arrival in Maumee City was found in their collection. Chief Justice Waite's grandson, also named Morrison R. Waite, of Cincinnati, Ohio, graciously consented to answer questions and wrote me concerning the "loving character" of his grandfather.

One full scale biography of the late Chief Justice has been published: TRIMBLE, BRUCE R. *Chief Justice Waite, Defender of the Public Interest*. Princeton: Princeton University Press, 1938. The following books also contain some useful information about Waite's career on the Court:

BATES, ERNEST S. *The Story of the Supreme Court*. New York: Bobbs-Merrill, 1936, Chapter 7.

Frankfurter, Felix. *The Commerce Clause Under Marshall, Taney, and Waite.* Chapel Hill: University of North Carolina Press, 1937, Chapter 3.

Lewis, William D. (ed.) *Great American Lawyers.* Philadelphia: John C. Winston, 1909, Vol. VII. The materials on Waite were written by one of his personal friends, Benjamin R. Cowen.

Stokes, A. P. *Memorials of Eminent Yale Men.* New York: Macmillan, 1914.

Umbreit, Kenneth B. *Our Eleven Chief Justices.* New York: Harper and Bros., 1938, Chapter 7.

Much information concerning the operation of the Waite Court is found in the following two items:

Fairman, Charles. *Mr. Justice Miller and the Supreme Court, 1862-1890.* Cambridge: Harvard University Press, 1939.

Fairman, Charles. "What Makes a Great Justice? Mr. Justice Bradley and the Supreme Court, 1870-1892," *Bacon Lectures.* Boston: Boston University Press, 1953, pp. 425-485.

Two reviews of Trimble's biography of Waite are particularly useful: Hurst, Willard. *Harvard Law Review,* LI, 1306-1310 and Hamilton, Walton. *Yale Law Journal,* XLVII, 846-852.

Biographical sketches, memorials, obituaries, etc. appear in a number of legal periodicals, some of which are no longer published. Some good brief materials are found in *Albany Law Journal,* Vol. IX; *Chicago Legal News,* Vol. VI; *Green Bag,* Vol. XIV, XV. A particularly good brief sketch of Waite's life and career is found in *Case and Comment,* VIII, no. 2, (July, 1901), 157-158. Another useful paper is Morgan, Mrs. Mathew S. (ed.). "How Morrison R. Waite Came to be Nominated Chief Justice of the United States," *Northwest Ohio Quarterly,* XXIII (Summer, 1951), 140-144.

THE CASE

The citation for *Reynolds* v. *United States* is 98 U.S. 145 (1878). *Munn* v. *Illinois* is cited as 94 U.S. 113 (1877). The citation for *Cleveland* v. *United States* is 329 U.S. 14 (1946).

There is an abundance of materials on the Mormons and the practice of polygamy, but relatively few commentaries on the court decisions. The following books contain useful information.

O'DEA, THOMAS F. *The Mormons.* Chicago: University of Chicago Press, 1957.

MULDER, WILLIAM and MORTENSEN, A. RUSSELL (eds.). *Among the Mormons.* New York: A. A. Knopf, 1958.

YOUNG, KIMBALL. *Isn't One Wife Enough?* New York: Henry Holt, 1954.

The following articles were also useful sources of information:

ANDERSEN, JERRY R. "Polygamy in Utah," *Utah Law Review,* V (Spring, 1957), 381-389.

Note. "Polygamy and the Conflict of Laws," *Yale Law Journal,* XXXII (1922-23), 471-477.

SMITH, JOSEPH. "Polygamy in the United States—Has It Political Significance?" *The North American Review,* CLXXVI (1903), 450-458.

SMOOT, REED. "The Passing of Polygamy," *The North American Review,* CLXXXVII (1908), 117-123.

ZOLLMAN, CARL. "Religious Liberty in American Law," in *Selected Essays on Constitutional Law.* Chicago: Foundation Press, 1938, pp. 1108-1150.

Extended commentaries on polygamy appeared in a number of contemporary journals at the turn of the century. See, in particular, *Arena,* XXVIII, 160-167; XXIX, 466-72; XXXVI, 497-507 and *Current Literature,* L, 289-292.

NOTES FOR CHAPTER 3

THE MAN

Although at least two biographies of Justice Harlan have been
in preparation for some time, no complete book length study has
yet appeared. The Harlan family papers have been in the custody
of two political scientists who are working on the biographies
and have not been used. However, materials drawn from these
papers have been relied on heavily. Some of Harlan's private
papers are on deposit at the University of Louisville Law School.
A few Harlan letters in the Library of Congress have been examined. In addition, the following materials were most useful in
preparing the sketch of his life:

ABRAHAM, HENRY J. "John Marshall Harlan: A Justice Neglected,"
    Virginia Law Review, XLI (November, 1955), 871-91.

BETH, LOREN P. "Justice Harlan and the Uses of Dissent," *Amer-
    ican Political Science Review*, XLIX (December, 1955), 1085-
    1104.

CLARK, FLOYD B. "The Constitutional Doctrines of Justice Har-
    lan." (Doctoral dissertation, studies in historical and political
    science) Baltimore: Johns Hopkins Press, 1915.

FARRELLY, DAVID G. "A Sketch of John Marshall Harlan's Pre-
    Court Career," *Vanderbilt Law Review*, X (February, 1957),
    209-225.

GILL, ROBERT L. "Defenders of Civil Liberties," *The Quarterly
    Review of Higher Education Among Negroes*, XVII (January,
    1949), 1-9.

HARLAN, RICHARD D. "Justice Harlan and the Game of Golf,"
    Scribner's Magazine, LXII (1917), 626-635.

LEWIS, ELLWOOD W. "Document, The Appointment of Mr. Justice
    Harlan," *Indiana Law Journal*, XXIX (Fall, 1953), 46-74.

STEIN, SIMON B. "John Marshall Harlan, the Great Dissenter," *Boston Bar Bulletin*, XXVI (October, 1955), 257-259.

WAITE, EDWARD F. "How 'Eccentric' was Mr. Justice Harlan?" *Minnesota Law Review*, XXXVII (February, 1953), 173-187.

WATT, RICHARD F. and ORLIKOFF, RICHARD M. "The Coming Vindication of Mr. Justice Harlan," *Illinois Law Review*, XLIV (March-April, 1949), 13-40.

WESTIN, ALAN F. "John Marshall Harlan and the Constitutional Rights of Negroes," *Yale Law Journal*, LXVI (April, 1957), 637-710.

The best collections of articles on Justice Harlan is found in *Kentucky Law Journal*, Vol. XLVI (Spring, 1958). Articles are written by Messrs. Abraham, Florian Bartosic, Farrelly and Westin. A good sketch of Harlan's life appears also in *Dictionary of American Biography*, VIII, 269-272.

THE CASE

The citation for *Plessy* v. *Ferguson* is 163 U.S. 537 (1896). In recent years there has been a veritable flood of materials on segregation appearing in the form of newspaper commentaries, magazine articles, books, pamphlets, and the like. Only a small portion of the most useful materials are noted below.

A starting point for any study involving the Negro in America is the following classic work: MYRDAL, GUNNAR. *An American Dilemma.* 2 vols. New York: Harper and Bros., 1944. Other useful materials are found in FRAZIER, E. FRANKLIN. *The Negro in the United States.* New York: Macmillan, 1957. KEY, V. O. JR. *Southern Politics in State and Nation.* New York: A. A. Knopf, 1950. "To Secure These Rights," (Report on the President's Committee on Civil Rights) Washington, D. C.: Government Printing Office, 1947.

For good materials on segregation see, in particular, HARLAN, LOUIS R. *Separate and Unequal*. Chapel Hill: University of North Carolina Press, 1958. HARRIS, ROBERT J. *The Quest for Equality*. Baton Rouge: Louisiana State University Press, 1960; NORDHOLT, J. W. SCHULTE. *The People Who Walk in Darkness*. London: Burke, 1960; WOODWARD, C. VANN. *The Strange Career of Jim Crow*. New York: Oxford University Press, 1957.

Good articles on segregation have appeared in *The Annals*, Vol. CCLXXV (May, 1951); *The Annals*, Vol. CCCIV (March, 1956). See also SMITH, LILLIAN. *Now is the Time*. New York: Dell Publishing Co., 1955. *Plessy* v. *Ferguson* is discussed in almost all the articles dealing with Justice Harlan cited above. In addition, good discussions are found in ROCHE, JOHN, P. "Plessy v. Ferguson: Requiescat in Pace?," *University of Penna. Law Review*, III (October, 1954), 44-58; WARNER, ROBERT M. "Detroit's First Supreme Court Justice," *Detroit Historical Society Bulletin*, XIII (May, 1957), 8-13.

Much has already been written on Chief Justice Warren, the Warren Court, and desegregation. The following items are most useful:

BERMAN, DANIEL. "Constitutional Issues and the Warren Court," *American Political Science Review*, LIII (June, 1959), 500-502.

BETH, LOREN P. "The Supreme Court and State Civil Liberties," *The Western Political Quarterly*, XIV (December, 1961), 825-838.

CHASE, HAROLD W. "The Warren Court and Congress," *Minnesota Law Review*, XLIV (1960), 595-637.

CHRISTMAN, HENRY, M. (ed.) *The Public Papers of Chief Justice Earl Warren*. New York: Simon and Schuster, 1959.

DILLIARD, IRVING. "Warren and the New Supreme Court," *Harper's Magazine*, December, 1955, pp. 59-64.

Editorial, "The New Chief Justice," *The Nation*, October 10, 1953, pp. 282-284.

FRANK, JOHN P. "Affirmative Opinion on Justice Warren," *New York Times Magazine*, October 3, 1954, p. 17.

GRESSMAN, EUGENE. "The Coming Trials of Justice Warren," *New Republic*, October 12, 1953, pp. 8-10.

HEYMAN, MICHAEL. "The Chief Justice, Racial Segregation, and the Friendly Critics," *California Law Review*, XLIX (March, 1961), 104-125.

JACOBS, CLYDE E. "The Warren Court—after Three Terms," *The Western Political Quarterly*, IX (December, 1956), 937-954.

PRITCHETT, C. HERMAN. "The Supreme Court and Our Civil Liberties," *The Nation*, October 9, 1954, pp. 302-305.

SCHWARTZ, BERNARD. "Warren Court—An Opinion," *New York Times Magazine*, June 30, 1957, p. 10.

VAREY, HAROLD L. "Earl Warren: Ike's Worst Appointment," *American Mercury*, August, 1958, pp. 5-13.

WARREN, EARL. Address, *The Law School Record*, University of Chicago, VII (1958), 7.

WARREN, EARL. "Blessings of Liberty," *Washington University Quarterly*, MCMLV (April, 1955), 105-111.

WARREN, EARL. "The Law and the Future," *Fortune*, November, 1955, p. 106.

WARREN, EARL. "The Years Ahead," *New York University Law Review*, XXXIV (November, 1959), 1161-1165.

YEAGER, P. and STIRK, J. "The Supreme Court in Transition," *New York Times Magazine*, March 10, 1957, p. 13.

ZIEGLER, B. M. (ed.). *Desegregation and the Supreme Court.* Boston: D. C. Heath, 1958.

NOTES FOR CHAPTER 4

The Man

The personal papers of Justice Holmes have been entrusted by the executors of the Holmes estate to Professor Mark De Wolfe Howe of the Harvard Law School who is preparing a biography of the Justice. The first volume of that biography has been published: *Justice Oliver Wendell Holmes: The Shaping Years (1841-1870)*. Cambridge: Harvard University Press, 1957. Other volumes are in preparation.

Two collections of letters under the editorship of Professor Howe are particularly useful for a student of Holmes' philosophy. These are: *Holmes–Laski letters, 1916-1935*. 2 vols. Cambridge: Harvard University Press, 1953; and *Holmes–Pollock Letters, 1874-1932*. 2 vols. Cambridge: Harvard University Press, 1941. A smaller number of letters to Dr. John C. H. Wu also have been utilized. These can be found in SHRINER, HARRY C. (ed.). *Justice Oliver Wendell Holmes: His Book Notices and Uncollected Letters and Papers*. New York: Central Book, 1936. See also HOLMES, OLIVER WENDELL. *Collected Legal Papers*. New York: Harcourt, Brace, 1920.

A number of books have been written about Holmes. The following have proved most useful.

BENT, SILAS. *Justice Oliver Wendell Holmes*. New York: Vanguard, 1932.

BIDDLE, FRANCIS. *Mr. Justice Holmes*. New York: Scribner's Sons, 1942.

BOWEN, CATHERINE D. *Yankee from Olympus: Justice Holmes and His Family*. Boston: Little, Brown, 1944.

FRANKFURTER, FELIX. *Mr. Justice Holmes and the Supreme Court*. Cambridge: Harvard University Press, 1938.

KONEFSKY, SAMUEL J. *The Legacy of Holmes and Brandeis*. New York: Macmillan, 1956.

LIEF, ALFRED. (ed.). *Dissenting Opinions of Mr. Justice Holmes*. New York: Vanguard, 1929.

MARKE, JULIUS J. (ed.). *The Holmes Reader*. Dobbs Ferry, N. Y.: Oceana, 1955.

LERNER, MAX. *The Mind and Faith of Mr. Justice Holmes*. Garden City, New York: Halycon House Reprint, 1948.

Among the hundreds of articles on Holmes the following were found to be particularly useful:

COHEN, MORRIS R. "Justice Holmes and the Nature of Law," *Columbia Law Review*, XXXI (March, 1931), 352-367.

FISCH, M. H. "Justice Holmes, the Prediction Theory of Law, and Pragmatism," *Journal of Philosophy*, XXXIX (February, 1942), 85-97.

GARRATY, JOHN A. "Holmes' Appointment to the U. S. Supreme Court," *The New England Quarterly* XXII (September, 1949), 291-303.

HOFSTADTER, SAMUEL H. "Mr. Justice Holmes: Exponent of Judicial Relativity," *American Bar Association Journal*, XLII (January, 1956), 19-23.

KRISLOV, SAMUEL. "Oliver Wendell Holmes: The Ebb and Flow of Judicial Legendry," *Northwestern Law Review*, LII (September-October, 1957), 514-525.

LOWRY, WALKER. "Mr. Justice Holmes: The Community vs. the Individual," *California Law Review*, XXXVI (September, 1948), 390-404.

MENDELSON, WALLACE. "Mr. Justice Holmes," *Minnesota Law Review*, XXXVI (March, 1952), 343-363.

RODELL, FRED. "Justice Holmes and his Hecklers," *Yale Law Journal*, LX (April, 1951), 620-624.

TUFTS, JAMES H. "The Legal and Social Philosophy of Mr. Justice Holmes," *American Bar Association Journal*, VII (July, 1921), 359-363.

Wyzanski, Charles E., Jr. "The Democracy of Justice Oliver Wendell Holmes," *Vanderbilt Law Review,* VII (April, 1954), 311-324.

Beginning in the early nineteen forties, the disciples of natural law began a concerted attack on the Holmes philosophy. They argued that his theories led directly to totalitarianism. Even the conservative columnist, Westbrook Pegler, entered the fray claiming that Holmes was nothing but a "cynical and senile brutalitarian" who believed that force alone "was the supreme force of civilization." The essence of the attack on Holmes is found in the following articles:

Gregg, Paul L. "The Pragmatism of Mr. Justice Holmes," *Georgetown Law Journal,* XXXI (March, 1943), 262-295.

Lucey, Francis E. "Jurisprudence and the Future of Social Order," *Social Science,* XVI (1941), 211.

Lucey, Francis E. "Holmes—Liberal—Humanitarian—Believer in Democracy," *Georgetown Law Journal,* XXXIX (May, 1951), 523-562.

Palmer, Benjamin W. "The Totalitarianism of Mr. Justice Holmes, *American Bar Association Journal,* XXXVII (November, 1951), 809-811. In a previous article in vol. XXXI, p. 569 of the same Journal, Palmer linked Holmes with Hobbes and Hitler.

The best reply to these remarks is the following: Howe, Mark De Wolfe. "The Positivism of Mr. Justice Holmes," *Harvard Law Review,* LXIV (February, 1951), 529-546. See also Biddle, Francis. *Justice Holmes, Natural Law and the Supreme Court.* New York: Macmillan, 1960.

A number of law reviews have dedicated specific issues to Justice Holmes. One of the best of these is the March, 1931 issue of the *Harvard Law Review,* Vol. XLIV, in celebration of Holmes' ninetieth birthday. In addition to a series of articles, the appendices contain a bibliography of the Justice's writings, opinions on the Massachusetts Supreme Court and opinions on the Supreme Court.

THE CASE

The decision of the District Court in the Schwimmer case was not reported. The Circuit Court of Appeals title and citation is *Schwimmer* v. *United States,* 27 Fed. (2d) 742 (1928). The Supreme Court title and citation is *United States* v. *Schwimmer,* 279 U. S. 644 (1929.) The citation for *Abrams* v. *United States* is 250 U. S. 616 (1919.)

The following articles provide additional background and comment on the case.

BROMLEY, DOROTHY D. "The Pacifist Bogey," *Harper's Magazine,* CLXI (1930), 553-566.

FALLON, PERLIE P. "Some Influences of Justice Holmes' Thought on Current Law: Assessments; Bankruptcy; Citizenship; Commerce," *Temple Law Quarterly,* March, 1945, pp. 15-25.

HAZARD, HENRY B. "Attachment to the Principles of the Constitution as Judicially Construed in Certain Naturalization Cases in the United States," *American Journal of International Law,* XXIII (October, 1929), 738-808.

HAZARD, HENRY B. Note, *American Journal of International Law,* XXIII (July, 1929), 626-632.

Note, "Effect of Woman Applicants' Expression of Unwillingness to Personally Bear Arms," *Virginia Law Review,* December, 1929, pp. 169-174.

PUGH, ROBERT C. "Pacifism and Citizenship—The Case of Rosika Schwimmer," *University of Cincinnati Law Review,* November, 1929, pp. 462-471.

A number of other law journals carried briefer notes on the case. Probably the most useful contemporary accounts of the case are found in *The New York Times,* which gave it sustained coverage from May 28, 1929 to June 8, 1929. Articles on Madame Schwimmer also appeared later in June. Other good brief accounts are found in *The Literary Digest* and *The Nation.*

NOTES FOR CHAPTER 5

THE MAN

The *Charles Evans Hughes Papers* in the Manuscript Division, Library of Congress, constitute the best single source of information on the late Chief Justice. I have perused only a small portion of this voluminous but carefully arranged collection. The *Papers* are still in the restricted category and may be examined only after permission is granted by the chief of the Manuscript Division.

The most complete published work on Hughes is the following Pulitzer prize-winning biography: PUSEY, MERLO J. *Charles Evans Hughes.* 2 Vols. New York: Macmillan, 1951. Pusey relied principally on the Hughes papers containing several hundred pages of biographical notes written by the Chief Justice after his retirement and on a number of interviews with Hughes and members of his family. The chief criticism of the work has been that it is too laudatory. There is a tendency to present Hughes as a superman.

Many interesting clippings on Hughes are found in the *Scrapbook of Justices,* collected by the Clerk's Office, Supreme Court, but now located (Volumes 1–14) in the National Archives.

The following books are also useful sources of information:

HENDEL, SAMUEL. *Charles Evans Hughes and the Supreme Court.* New York: Kings' Crown Press, Columbia University, 1951.

PERKINS, DEXTER. *Charles Evans Hughes and American Democratic Statesmanship*. Boston: Little, Brown, 1956.

RANSOM, WILLIAM L. *Charles Evans Hughes, The Statesman as Shown in the Opinions of the Jurist*. New York: E. P. Dutton, 1916.

STONE, IRVING. *They Also Run* Book III, Chapter 2. Garden City, N. Y.: Doubleday, 1946.

Much is revealed about Hughes in his own collection of six lectures on the Supreme Court given at Columbia University and appearing in *The Supreme Court of the United States*. Garden City, N. Y.: Garden City Publishing Co., 1936.

Also useful are the proceedings of the Supreme Court in memory of Chief Justice Hughes in 338 U. S. XIII-XXVIII, 1948, 1949. A readable account of the Court's struggle with President Franklin D. Roosevelt in 1937 is ALSOP, JOSEPH and CATLEDGE, TURNER. *The 168 Days*. Garden City, N. Y.: Doubleday, Doran, 1938.

The following articles were also utilized in preparing the chapter:

CHAFEE, ZECHARIAH, Jr. "Charles Evans Hughes," *Proceedings of the American Philosophical Society*, XCIII (1949), 267-281.

ELLISTON, HERBERT. "The Integrity of Justice Hughes," *The Atlantic*, April, 1952, pp. 73-75.

FRANKFURTER, FELIX and McELWAIN, EDWIN. "The 'Administrative Side' of Chief Justice Hughes; the Business of the Supreme Court as Conducted by Chief Justice Hughes," *Harvard Law Review*, LXIII (November, 1949), 1-26.

HENDEL, SAMUEL. "The 'Liberalism' of Chief Justice Hughes," *Vanderbilt Law Review*, X (February, 1957), 259-268.

MASON, ALPHEUS T. "Charles Evans Hughes: An Appeal to the Bar of History," *Vanderbilt Law Review*, VI (December, 1952), 1-19.

PRINGLE, HENRY F. "Chief Justice," *Essay Annual*, ed. ERICH A. WALTER. Chicago: Scott, Foresman, 1936, pp. 121-150. Reprint of articles appearing in *The New Yorker*, June 29, July 6, July 13, 1935.

RIBBLE, F. D. G. "The Constitutional Doctrines of Chief Justice Hughes," *Columbia Law Review*, XLI (November, 1941), 1190-1215. This article contains a useful appendix of all cases in which an opinion was written by Hughes while serving as Chief Justice.

WARREN, EARL. "Charles Evans Hughes and the Spirit of Tolerance," *Representative American Speeches: 1956-1957*, ed. A. CRAIG BAIRD. New York: H. W. Wilson, 1957, pp. 135-140.

THE CASE

The citation for *United States* v. *Macintosh* is 283 U. S. 605 (1931). The title and citation in the Court of Appeals is *United States* v. *Macintosh*, 42F (2d) 845 (1930). Two other cases referred to in the narrative are *United States* v. *Bland*, 283 U. S. 636 (1931) and *Girouard* v. *United States*, 328 U. S. 61 (1946).

The following articles were most useful in preparing the case discussion:

Editorial, "The Supreme Court Violates the Constitution," *The Christian Century*, June 17, 1931, pp. 798-800.

GRAY, HERMAN A. "Willingness to Bear Arms as a Prerequisite to Naturalization," *New York University Law Quarterly*, XII (March, 1930), 723-727.

HALE, RICHARD W. "Letter on Macintosh Case Symposium," *Illinois Law Review*, XXVI (February, 1932), 681-683.

LUCCOCK, HALFORD E. "Douglas Clyde Macintosh," *The Christian Century*, January 20, 1932, pp. 87-89.

Note, "The Macintosh Case," *Yale Law Review*, XL (1930-31), 653-657.

Note, "Citizenship Properly Denied to one Who Will Not Accept the Oath of Allegiance without Qualification as to service in War," *Law and Labor*, XXXI (1931), 159-163.

Ross, J. ELLIOT. "Conscience and the State, the Roman Catholic View," *The Christian Century,* January 20, 1932, pp. 86-87.

WIGMORE, JOHN H., SEARS, KENNETH C., FREUND, ERNST, and GREEN, FREDERICK. "United States Vs. Macintosh—A Symposium," *Illinois Law Review,* XXVI (December, 1931), 375-396. Reprinted in *Selected Essays on Constitutional Law.* Vol. 2. Chicago: Foundation Press, 1938, pp. 1265-1285.

A number of other comments appeared in *Christian Century* during 1931 and 1932. Interesting reader comment is found in the July 1, 1931 issue, pp. 878-879. Among contemporary popular journals most extensive coverage was given the case by *The Literary Digest.* See, in particular, the following issues: July 13, 1929, p. 12; January 23, 1930, p. 14; July 12, 1930, p. 7; June 6, 1931, p. 7. A good discussion of both the Schwimmer and Macintosh cases appears in CHAFEE, ZECHARIAH, JR. *Free Speech in the United States.* Cambridge: Harvard University Press, 1942, pp. 366-375.

NOTES FOR CHAPTER 6

THE MAN

The following two books are most useful in studying the life and early judicial work of Justice Black.

FRANK, JOHN P. *Mr. Justice Black: The Man and His Opinions.* New York: A. A. Knopf, 1949.

WILLIAMS, CHARLOTTE. *Hugo L. Black, a Study in the Judicial Process.* Baltimore: Johns Hopkins Press, 1950.

Justice Black's Constitutional philosophy is explored thoroughly in MENDELSON, WALLACE. *Justices Black and Frankfurter: Conflict in the Court.* Chicago: University of Chicago Press, 1961. See

174

References

also a review of the book by Rocco J. Tresolini in *American Political Science Review*, LV (1961), 403.

A readable brief sketch of Black's life and early work on the Court appears in McCune, Wesley. *"The Nine Young Men*. New York: Harper and Bros., 1947, pp. 26-46.

Justice Black has been the subject of a great number of articles. Black's early life and background are well presented in Childers, James S. "Hugo Black, Always an Alabamian," *The Birmingham News–Age–Herald*, January 31, 1937, p. 3. A number of articles concerning Black's early life and controversial appointment to the Court appeared in a number of periodicals, particularly *The Nation* and *The New Republic* between 1937-1940. A longtime admirer of Justice Black, Max Lerner, wrote the best of these articles for *The Nation*. Another useful source is Shankweiler, Anna G. "The Life and Times of Associate Justice Hugo La Fayette Black." Unpublished Master's thesis, Lehigh University, 1943.

The following additional articles have been extremely useful:

Armstrong, Walter P. "Mr. Justice Black" (a Review of Frank's book cited above), *Tennessee Law Review*, XX (April, 1949), 638-643.

Barnett, Vincent M. Jr. "Mr. Justice Black and the Supreme Court," *University of Chicago Law Review*, VIII (December, 1940), 20-41.

Berman, Daniel M. "Hugo L. Black: The Early Years," *Catholic University of America Law Review*, VIII (May, 1959), 103-116.

Bickel, Alexander M. "Mr. Justice Black, The Unobvious Meaning of Plain Words," *The New Republic*, CXLII (March 14, 1960), 13-15.

Black, Charles L., Jr. "Justice Black, the Supreme Court, and the Bill of Rights," *Harper's*, CCXXII (February, 1961), 63-68.

Gill, Robert L. "Defenders of Civil Liberties," *Quarterly Review of Higher Education Among Negroes*, XVII (January, 1949), 1-9.

References   175

LEWIS, ANTHONY. "Justice Black at 75: Still the Dissenter," *The New York Times Magazine*, February 26, 1961, pp. 13, 73-75.

MADISON, CHARLES A. "Justice Hugo Black: Still Dissenting at 70," *The Nation*, CLXXXII (January 25, 1956), 156-158.

MENDELSON, WALLACE. "Mr. Justice Black and the Rule of Law," *Midwest Journal of Political Science*, IV (August, 1960), 250-266.

RODELL, FRED. "Justice Hugo Black," *The American Mercury*, LIX (August, 1944), 135-143.

WEISSMAN, DAVID L. and GORDON, MURRAY A. "Mr. Justice Black at 70," *Lawyers Guild Review*, XVI (Fall, 1956), 101-103.

Yale Law Journal, LXV (February, 1956), 449-558, is largely devoted to articles on Justice Black on the occasion of his seventieth birthday.

THE CASE

The citation for *Chambers* v. *Florida* is 309 U. S. 227 (1940). The title and citation for the five appeals to the Florida Supreme Court are as follows:

1. *Chambers* et al. v. *State*, 111 Fla. 707, 151. So. 499 (1933)
2. *Chambers* et al. v. *State*, 111 Fla. 707, 152 So. 437 (1934)
3. *Chambers* et al. v. *State*, 117 Fla. 642, 158 So. 153 (1934)
4. *Chambers* et al. v. *State*, 123 Fla. 734, 167 So. 697 (1936)
5. *Chambers* et al. v. *State*, 136 Fla. 568, 187 So. 156 (1939)

Brief comments on the Chambers case are found in numerous works on American constitutional law and constitutional history. In addition the following brief commentaries are particularly useful.

Note, *Michigan Law Rev.*, XXXVIII (1940), 858-863.
Note, *Michigan Law Rev.*, XXXIX (1940), 274-283.
Note, *Temple University Law Q.*, XIV (April, 1940), 404-406.

Note, *Washington Law Rev. and State Bar. Jour.,* XV (July, 1940), 186-187.

For descriptions of the four defendants and for other materials that do not appear in the written record of the case I am indebted to Mr. Sidney J. Catts, Jr., a lawyer from West Palm Beach, Florida, who represented the defendants in the trial court after the fourth appeal to the Florida Supreme Court. I am also grateful to Mr. Richard W. Ervin, Attorney General of Florida in 1960, who also helped me obtain additional information about the case.

NOTES FOR CHAPTER 7

The Man

The best full-length study of Justice Murphy to date is Woodford, Howard J. Jr. "Frank Murphy: A Liberal's Creed." Unpublished Ph.D. dissertation, Department of Politics, Princeton University, 1959. I am grateful to Dr. Howard for allowing me to use his copy of the thesis over an extended period of time. I have drawn heavily from his findings.

The other major source of information on Murphy is the articles written by Eugene Gressman, a practicing attorney in Washington, who served as Murphy's law clerk for five years. Gressman's articles are invaluable since he has been able to utilize the Murphy papers entrusted to him by the family of the late Justice. To date, other researchers have not had access to these papers. His important studies are the following: "Mr. Justice Murphy—A Preliminary Appraisal," *Columbia Law Review.* L (January, 1950), 29-47, and "The Controversial Image of Mr. Justice Murphy," *Georgetown Law Journal,* XLVII (Summer, 1959), 631-654.

A good sketch of Murphy's life is found in 340 U. S. V-XXV (1950). Another briefer sketch, evidently based on rather flimsy evidence, is SCHLESINGER, ARTHUR M. JR. "The Supreme Court 1947," *Fortune,* January, 1947, pp. 73, 76. A more reliable sketch is found in McCUNE, WESLEY, *The Nine Young Men.* New York: Harper and Bros., 1947, pp. 137-151.

The *Michigan Law Review,* XLVIII (April, 1950), 737-810 is dedicated to the memory of Justice Murphy. A note of appreciation by Murphy's three law clerks and articles by Thurgood Marshall and Archibald Cox are particularly useful.

The following articles were also valuable in preparing the sketch of Justice Murphy:

ARNOLD, THURMAN. "Mr. Justice Murphy," *Harvard Law Review,* LXIII (December, 1949), 689-693.

BARNETT, VINCENT M. JR. "Mr. Justice Murphy, Civil Liberties and the Holmes Tradition," *Cornell Law Quarterly* XXXII (November, 1946), 177-221.

FAHY, CHARLES. "The Judicial Philosophy of Mr. Justice Murphy," *Yale Law Journal,* LX (May, 1951), 812-820.

FRANK, JOHN P. "Justice Murphy: The Goals Attempted," *Yale Law Journal,* LI (December, 1949), 1-26.

MAN, ALBON P. JR. "Mr. Justice Murphy and the Supreme Court," *Virginia Law Review,* XXXVI (November, 1950), 889-943.

ROCHE, JOHN P. "The Utopian Pilgrimage of Mr. Justice Murphy," *Vanderbilt Law Review,* X (February, 1957), 369-394.

SCANLAN, ALFRED T. "The Passing of Justice Murphy—The Conscience of the Court," *Notre Dame Lawyer,* XXV (Fall, 1949), 4-35.

WEISS, LEO. "Justice Murphy and the Welfare Question," *Michigan Law Review,* LIII (February, 1955), 541-566.

The following books also contain useful information on Justice Murphy:

GERHART, EUGENE C. *Robert Jackson: America's Advocate.* Indianapolis and New York: Bobbs-Merrill, 1958.

PRITCHETT, C. HERMAN. *The Roosevelt Court*. New York: Macmillan, 1948.

MASON, ALPHEUS T. *Harlan Fiske Stone: Pillar of the Law*, New York: Viking Press, 1956.

THE CASE

The citation for *Korematsu* v. *United States* is 323 U. S. 214 (1944). *Hirabayashi* v. *United States* is cited as 320 U. S. 81 (1943). The citation for *Ex parte Endo* is 323 U. S. 283 (1944).

A great deal has been written about the exclusion of the Japanese-Americans from the west coast. Only a portion of the most widely utilized materials are cited here.

Useful government publications include the following: U. S. Army, Western Defense Command and Fourth Army. *Final Report: Japanese Evacuation from the West Coast*, Washington, D. C.: Government Printing Office, 1942; three publications by the War Relocation Authority, U. S. Department of Interior, published in 1946 by the Government Printing Office and entitled as follows:

1. *The Wartime Handling of Evacuee Property.*
2. *The Evacuated People, a Quantitative Description.*
3. *Wartime Exile, The Exclusion of Japanese Americans from the West Coast.*

A three-volume extensive study of the entire evacuation and resettlement program has been published by the University of California Press, Berkeley and Los Angeles. Authors and titles are as follows: THOMAS, DOROTHY S. and NISHIMOTO, RICHARD S. *The Spoilage*, 1946; THOMAS, DOROTHY SWAINE. *The Salvage*, 1952; TEN BROEK, JACOBUS, BARNHART, EDWARD N., and MATSON, FLOYD W., *Prejudice, War and the Constitution*, 1954.

Two other most useful books are GRODZINS, MORTON. *Americans Betrayed*. Chicago: University of Chicago Press, 1949, and

LEIGHTON, ALEXANDER H. *The Governing of Men*. Princeton: Princeton University Press, 1945.

The most widely used articles were the following:

ALEXANDRE, MAURICE. "*Wartime Control of Japanese—Americans*," *Cornell Law Quarterly*, XXVIII (June, 1943), 385-413.

DEMBITZ, NANETTE. "Racial Discrimination and the Military Judgment," *Columbia Law Review*, XLV (March, 1945), 175-239.

DUSENBERY, VERNE, *et al.* "The Japanese Problem in Oregon," *Oregon Law Review*, XXIV (April, 1945), 208-219.

FREEMAN, HARROP A. "Genesis, Exodus and Leviticus—Genealogy, Evacuation, and Law," *Cornell Law Quarterly*, XXVIII (June, 1943), 414-458.

ROSTOW, EUGENE V. "The Japanese American Cases—A Disaster," *Yale Law Journal*, LIV (June, 1945), 489-533. A popularized version of this article entitled "Our Worst Wartime Mistake," appeared in *Harper's Magazine*, CXCI (September, 1945), 193-201.

WOLFSON, RICHARD F. "Legal Doctrine, War Power and Japanese Evacuation," *Kentucky Law Journal*, XXXII (May, 1944), 328-342.

Some useful information was obtained from *The Commonwealth*, March 10, 1944, which is devoted largely to the Japanese-Americans and from an article in *Fortune*, XXIX (April, 1944), p. 8, entitled "Issei, Nisei, Kibei."

NOTES FOR CHAPTER 8

THE MAN

No complete biography of Justice Rutledge has been written. The most useful accounts of various aspects of his life and work may be found in the following articles:

"In Memory of Honorable Wiley Rutledge," Proceedings Before United States Supreme Court, *Iowa Law Review*, XXXVI (Summer, 1951), 591-606.

CANON, ALFRED O. "Mr. Justice Rutledge and the Roosevelt Court," *Vanderbilt Law Review*, X (February, 1957), 167-192.

EDGERTON, HENRY W. "Mr. Justice Rutledge," *Harvard Law Review*, LXIII (December, 1949), 293-298.

FORRESTER, RAY. "Mr. Justice Rutledge—A New Factor," *Tulane Law Review*, XVII (April, 1943), 511-536.

FUCHS, RALPH F. "The Judicial Art of Wiley B. Rutledge," *Washington University Law Quarterly*, XXVIII (April, 1945), 115-146.

ICKES, I. H. "Justice Rutledge," *New Republic*, September 26, 1949, p. 20.

LEVITAN, DAVID M. "Mr. Justice Rutledge," *Virginia Law Review*, XXXIV (May-June, 1948), 393-416, 526-552.

MASHER, LESTER E. "Mr. Justice Rutledge's Philosophy of Civil Rights," *New York University Law Quarterly Review*, XXIV (October, 1949), 661-706.

MENDELSON, WALLACE. "Mr. Justice Rutledge's Mark upon the Bill of Rights," *Columbia Law Review*, L (January, 1950), 48-51.

ROCKWELL, LANDON G. "Justice Rutledge on Civil Liberties," *Yale Law Journal*, LIX (December, 1949), 27-59.

The best collection of articles on Justice Rutledge is found in a symposium to his memory in *Iowa Law Review*, XXXV (Sum-

mer, 1950), 541-699. A good brief sketch of his life is found in
DUNHAM, A. and KURLAND, P. B. (eds.). *Mr. Justice.* Chicago:
University of Chicago Press, 1956, pp. 177-202. Another brief
sketch appears in McCUNE, WESLEY. *The Nine Young Men,* New
York: Harper and Bros., 1947, Chapter 16.

THE CASE

The trial record of the Yamashita case has never been printed
and can be read in transcript form only in the National Archives
and Records Service in Washington, D. C. Extra copies of the
transcript are not available. Microfilm copies of the transcript
and exhibits can be made at a cost of approximately $500. The
trial record consists of thirty-four volumes totaling 4,063 pages.
There are 437 exhibits.

The title and citation of the Supreme Court decision in the case
is *In re Yamashita,* 327 United States 1 (1946). REEL, A. FRANK.
The Case of General Yamashita. Chicago: University of Chicago
Press, 1949, is the best single source of information on the case
and on the life and background of General Yamashita. Another
defense lawyer's useful recollections of the case are found in
FELDHAUS, J. GORDON. "The Trial of Yamashita," *South Dakota
Bar Journal,* XV (October, 1946), 181-193.

Other worthwhile comments are found in GANOE, JOHN T. "The
Yamashita Case and the Constitution," *Oregon Law Review,* XXV
(April, 1946), 143-158. The whole problem of military jurisdiction is reviewed thoroughly in FAIRMAN, CHARLES. "The Supreme
Court on Military Jurisdiction: Martial Rule in Hawaii and the
Yamashita Case," *Harvard Law Review,* LIX (July, 1946), 833-
883. A good brief comment is the following note on trials of
enemy combatants after hostilities in BRADY, L. B. Note, *Michigan Law Review,* XLIV (April, 1946), 855-861. See, also, the
note entitled "Judicial Review of War Crime Trials," *Illinois Law
Review,* XL (March-April, 1946), 546-553.

Many newspapers and magazines carried brief but colorful comments and reports on the Yamashita case. The best of these are found in *Time, Newsweek,* and *New Republic.*

Most helpful in obtaining perspective for this Chapter was an interview in New York City on March 22, 1961, with Mr. A. Frank Reel, Yamashita's dedicated defense lawyer, who still has a vivid recollection of the case.

NOTES FOR EPILOGUE

The citations for the Shipp case are as follows: *United States v. Shipp,* 203 U.S. 563 (1906); 214 U.S. 386 (1909). A good brief discussion of the case appears in KING, WILLARD L. *Melville Weston Fuller.* New York: Macmillan Co., 1950, pp. 323-327. The various volumes of the *Scrapbook of Justices* in the Justice and Executive Branch of the National Archives contain numerous newspaper clippings on the case. These provided additional factual information. Most useful were clippings from the following newspapers. *Chattanooga Times,* Tuesday, May 25, 1909, January 31, 1910; *Knoxville Sentinel,* January 31, 1910; *New York Sun,* November 16, 1909, November 18, 1909; *New York World,* November 17, 1909, November 21, 1909, January 31, 1910; *Washington Herald,* June 2, 1909, November 28, 1909; *Washington Post,* November 16, 1909, January 30, 1910; *Washington Times,* May 3, 1909, December 25, 1909, January 29, 1910.

APPENDIX 1

Civil Rights in the Constitution

FIRST TEN AMENDMENTS (ADOPTED IN 1791)

Amendment I

Congress shall make no law respecting an establishment of religion, or prohibiting the free exercise thereof; or abridging the freedom of speech, or of the press; or the right of the people peaceably to assemble and to petition the Government for a redress of grievances.

Amendment II

A well-regulated militia being necessary to the security of a free State, the right of the people to keep and bear arms, shall not be infringed.

AMENDMENT III

No soldier shall, in time of peace, be quartered in any house without the consent of the owner, nor in time of war but in a manner to be prescribed by law.

AMENDMENT IV

The right of the people to be secure in their persons, houses, papers, and effects, against unreasonable searches and seizures, shall not be violated, and no warrants shall issue but upon probable cause, supported by oath or affirmation, and particularly describing the place to be searched, and the persons or things to be seized.

AMENDMENT V

No person shall be held to answer for a capital, or otherwise infamous crime, unless on a presentment or indictment of a Grand Jury, except in cases arising in the land or naval forces, or in the militia, when in actual service in time of war or public danger; nor shall any person be subject for the same offense to be twice put in jeopardy of life or limb; nor shall be compelled in any criminal case to be a witness against himself, nor be deprived of life, liberty, or property, without due process of law; nor shall private property be taken for public use, without just compensation.

AMENDMENT VI

In all criminal prosecutions, the accused shall enjoy the right to a speedy and public trial, by an impartial jury of the State and district wherein the crime shall have been committed, which districts shall have been previously ascertained by law, and to be informed of the nature and cause of the accusation; to be confronted with the witnesses against him; to have compulsory process for obtaining witnesses in his favor, and to have the assistance of counsel for his defense.

AMENDMENT VII

In suits at common law, where the value in controversy shall exceed twenty dollars, the right of trial by jury shall be preserved, and no fact tried by a jury, shall be otherwise re-examined in any court of the United States, than according to the rules of the common law.

AMENDMENT VIII

Excessive bail shall not be required, nor excessive fines imposed, nor cruel and unusual punishments inflicted.

AMENDMENT IX

The enumeration in the Constitution of certain rights shall not be construed to deny or disparage others retained by the people.

AMENDMENT X

The powers not delegated to the United States by the Constitution, nor prohibited by it to the States, are reserved to the States respectively, or to the people.

OTHER AMENDMENTS

Amendment XIII

1. Neither slavery nor involuntary servitude, except as a punishment for crime whereof the party shall have been duly convicted, shall exist within the United States, or any place subject to their jurisdiction.

2. Congress shall have power by appropriate legislation, to enforce the provisions of this article.

Amendment XIV

1. All persons born or naturalized in the United States, and subject to the jurisdiction thereof, are citizens of the United States and of the State wherein they reside. No State shall make or enforce any law which shall abridge the privileges or immunities of citizens of the United States, nor shall any State deprive any person of life, liberty, or property, without due process of law, nor deny to any person within its jurisdiction the equal protection of the laws. . . .

5. The Congress shall have power to enforce by appropriate legislation the provisions of this article.

Amendment XV

1. The right of citizens of the United States to vote shall not be denied or abridged by the United States or by any State on account of race, color, or previous condition of servitude.

2. The Congress shall have power to enforce this article by appropriate legislation.

Amendment XIX

1. The right of citizens of the United States to vote shall not be denied or abridged by the United States or by any State on account of sex.

2. Congress shall have power to enforce this article by appropriate legislation.

PROVISIONS FROM ORIGINAL CONSTITUTION

Article I

Section 9. . . .

2. The privilege of the writ of habeas corpus shall not be suspended, unless when in cases of rebellion or invasion the public safety may require it.

3. No bill of attainder or ex post facto law shall be passed.
Section 10.

1. No State shall . . . pass any bill of attainder, ex post facto law, or law impairing the obligation of contracts. . . .

Article III

Section 2. . . .

3. The trial of all crimes, except in cases of impeachment, shall be by jury. . . .
Section 3.

1. Treason against the United States shall consist only in levying war against them, or in adhering to their enemies, giving them aid and comfort. No Person shall be convicted of treason

unless on the testimony of two witnesses to the same overt act, or on confession in open court.

Article IV

Section 2.
1. The citizens of each State shall be entitled to all privileges and immunities of citizens in the several States.

Article VI

3. . . . no religious test shall ever be required as a qualification to any office or public trust under the United States.

APPENDIX 2

United States Supreme Court

Name	Term of Office
JOHN JAY	1780-1795
John Rutledge	1789-1791
William Cushing	1789-1810
James Wilson	1789-1798
John Blair	1789-1796
Robert H. Harrison	1789-1790
James Iredell	1790-1799
Thomas Johnson	1791-1793
William Paterson	1793-1806
JOHN RUTLEDGE	1795 [1]
Samuel Chase	1796-1811
OLIVER ELLSWORTH	1796-1799

[1] John Rutledge's appointment as Chief Justice in 1795 was not confirmed by Congress.

Name	Term of Office
Bushrod Washington	1798-1829
Alfred Moore	1799-1804
JOHN MARSHALL	1801-1835
William Johnson	1804-1834
Brockholst Livingston	1806-1823
Thomas Todd	1807-1826
Joseph Story	1811-1845
Gabriel Duval	1812-1835
Smith Thompson	1823-1843
Robert Trimble	1826-1828
John McLean	1829-1861
Henry Baldwin	1830-1844
James M. Wayne	1835-1867
ROGER B. TANEY	1836-1864
Philip P. Barbour	1836-1841
John Catron	1837-1865
John McKinley	1837-1852
Peter V. Daniel	1841-1860
Samuel Nelson	1845-1872
Levi Woodbury	1845-1851
Robert C. Grier	1846-1870
Benj. R. Curtis	1851-1857
John A. Campbell	1853-1861
Nathan Clifford	1858-1881
Noah H. Swayne	1862-1881
Samuel F. Miller	1862-1890
David Davis	1862-1877
Stephen J. Field	1863-1897
SALMON P. CHASE	1864-1873
William Strong	1870-1880
Joseph P. Bradley	1870-1892
Ward Hunt	1873-1882
MORRISON R. WAITE	1874-1888
John M. Harlan	1877-1911

Name	*Term of Office*
William B. Woods	1881-1887
Stanley Matthews	1881-1889
Horace Gray	1882-1902
Samuel Blatchford	1882-1893
Lucius Q. C. Lamar	1888-1893
MELVILLE W. FULLER	1888-1910
David J. Brewer	1890-1910
Henry B. Brown	1891-1906
George Shiras, Jr.	1892-1903
Howell E. Jackson	1893-1895
Edward D. White	1894-1910
Rufus W. Peckham	1896-1909
Joseph McKenna	1898-1925
Oliver W. Holmes, Jr.	1902-1932
William R. Day	1903-1922
William H. Moody	1906-1910
Horace H. Lurton	1910-1914
Charles E. Hughes	1910-1916
Willis Van Devanter	1911-1937
Joseph R. Lamar	1911-1916
EDWARD D. WHITE	1910-1921
Mahlon Pitney	1912-1922
James C. McReynolds	1914-1941
Louis D. Brandeis	1916-1939
John H. Clarke	1916-1922
WILLIAM H. TAFT	1921-1930
George Sutherland	1922-1938
Pierce Butler	1923-1939
Edward T. Sanford	1923-1930
Harlan F. Stone	1925-1941
CHARLES E. HUGHES	1930-1941
Owen J. Roberts	1930-1945
Benjamin N. Cardozo	1932-1938
Hugo L. Black	1937-

Name	Term of Office
Stanley F. Reed	1938-1957
Felix Frankfurter	1939-1962
William O. Douglas	1939-
Frank Murphy	1940-1949
HARLAN F. STONE	1941-1946
James F. Byrnes	1941-1942
Robert H. Jackson	1941-1954
Wiley B. Rutledge	1943-1949
Harold H. Burton	1945-1958
FREDERICK M. VINSON	1946-1953
Tom C. Clark	1949-
Sherman Minton	1949-1956
EARL WARREN	1953-
John M. Harlan	1955-
William J. Brennan, Jr.	1956-
Charles E. Whittaker	1957-1962
Potter Stewart	1958-
Byron R. White	1962-
Arthur J. Goldberg	1962-

APPENDIX 3

How the Supreme Court Decides Cases

The Supreme Court's annual term runs from the first Monday in October to the following June. After adjournment, special sessions may be called by the Chief Justice to consider questions of exceptional importance and urgency. For example, a special session was called in the summer of 1942 to deal with the case of German saboteurs. During the first week of the term the Court usually disposes of work which has accumulated over the summer months. After that the Court divides its time between the hearing of cases and recesses. The general pattern is for the Court to hear oral argument for two weeks and then to recess for two weeks to study cases and write opinions. Decisions are announced at noon on Mondays following the two weeks of argument. Many cases are disposed of in per curiam opinions, which are simply brief announcements, without full explanation, of the decision reached by the Court itself, rather than through the written

This material is from Rocco J. Tresolini, *American Constitutional Law* (New York: Macmillan, 1959), pp. 37-42. Reprinted by permission.

opinion of one of its members. A per curiam opinion may state simply that "the appeal is dismissed for want of a substantial federal question."

The method of disposing of cases by full opinion has remained substantially the same over a number of years. The procedure followed may be outlined briefly as follows:

(1). Cases filed in the Supreme Court are first placed on one of three dockets. The most important of these is the Appellate Docket, which consists of cases that have come from the lower courts for review. The few cases in which the original jurisdiction of the Court is invoked are placed on the Original Docket. The Miscellaneous Docket, which was created in 1945, comprises a wide variety of petitions, including a large number coming from prisoners who seek to challenge the legality of their convictions. Applications for the extraordinary writs such as mandamus and habeas corpus are also placed on the Miscellaneous Docket.

(2). The party bringing the action before the Supreme Court must file a brief, usually within forty-five days after the case has been placed on the docket. Thirty days later the answering brief must be filed by the other contending party. When the case comes before the Court on a writ of certiorari, the party bringing the action is called the petitioner, with the answering party known as the respondent. In appeal cases, the appellant brings the action, with the other party being referred to as the appellee. Forty copies of the brief must be filed with the Clerk of the Supreme Court by counsel for each party. The brief, which is filed in accordance with prescribed form, generally states the issues of the case, the questions presented, actions of the lower courts, and all necessary legal arguments with the citation of cases and statutes relied upon. A brief may also be filed by a person who is not a party to the case and is known as *amicus curiae,* or friend of the court. For example, the Solicitor General of the United States may file a brief as a friend of the court if a case involves issues of direct interest or concern to the federal government.

(3). All the briefs filed are studied by each of the justices with the aid of their respective law clerks. The decision as to whether or not oral arguments need to be heard is made after the briefs and other pertinent materials have been analyzed thoroughly. The maximum time allowed for oral argument is usually one hour for each of the contending parties. During the oral presentation, the justices may ask questions or request additional data on pertinent points of the case.

(4). After all the written and oral arguments have been presented, the justices meet in conference to vote on the case. These conferences are held each Friday morning while the Court is sitting. All the discussions are private, with only the members of the Court allowed in the conference room. What actually takes place at the conference can be determined only by the few comments that the justices themselves have made. However, it is known that the conference procedure does not vary greatly from year to year. Justice Stone once described the work of the conference as follows:

> On the day before the conference each judge receives a list of cases which will be taken up at the conference, and the order in which they will be considered. This list actually includes every case argued the day before the conference and all pending motions and applications for certiorari.
>
> At conference each case is presented for discussion by the Chief Justice, usually by a brief statement of the facts, the questions of law involved, and with such suggestions for their disposition as he may think appropriate. No cases have been assigned to any particular judge in advance of the conference. Each justice is prepared to discuss the case at length and to give his views as to the proper solution of the questions presented. In Mr. Justice Holmes' pungent phrase, each must be ready to "recite" on the case. Each judge is requested by the Chief Justice, in the order of seniority, to give his views and the conclusions which he has reached. The discussion is of the freest character and at the end, after full opportunity has been given for each member of the Court to be heard and for the asking and answering of questions, the vote is taken and recorded in the reverse order of the discussion, the youngest, in point of service, voting first.

On the same evening, after the conclusion of the conference, each member of the Court receives at his home a memorandum from the Chief Justice advising him of the assignment of cases for opinions. Opinions are written for the most part in recess, and as they are written they are printed and circulated among the justices, who make suggestions for their correction and revision. At the next succeeding conference these suggestions are brought before the full conference and accepted or rejected as the case may be. On the following Monday the opinion is announced by the writer as the opinion of the Court.

In addition to the majority decision of the Court, separate concurring and dissenting opinions may be written, although concurrence or dissent may be expressed without written opinion. Any justice is free to write a separate opinion if he is not satisfied with the majority decision. A concurring opinion is one which agrees with the Court's decision but disagrees with the reasoning by which the decision was reached. Dissenting opinions may be written when one or more of the justices disagrees with the decision of the Court as well as with the reasoning used in reaching the decision. Important concurring and dissenting opinions are useful for the student of government, as they may help clarify the majority opinion of the Court and reveal the important political, social, and economic conflicts involved in the case. As Professor Loren P. Beth has noted, the dissenting opinion "provides an argument opposing that of the majority which may be seized upon by lawyers and urged in succeeding cases with some hope of success. It calls attention to defects in the position of the majority forcing a rethinking and perhaps strengthening of that position. It further calls the majority to the bar of public opinion and enlightened legal opinion." [1] However, dissenting opinions may obscure as well as clarify the basic issues.

The technique of the dissenter often is to exaggerate the holding of the Court beyond the meaning of the majority and then to blast away at the excess. . . . Then, too, dissenters frequently force the majority to take positions more extreme than was originally intended. The

[1] Loren P. Beth, "Justice Harlan and the Uses of Dissent," *American Political Science Review,* XLIX (December, 1955), 1104.

classic example is the Dred Scott case, in which Chief Justice Taney's extreme statements were absent in his original draft and were inserted only after Mr. Justice McLean, then a more than passive candidate for the presidency, raised the issue in dissent. The right of dissent is a valuable one. Wisely used on well-chosen occasions, it has been of great service to the profession and to the law. . . . The tradition of great dissents built around such names as Holmes, Brandeis, Cardozo, and Stone is not due to the frequency or multiplicity of their dissents, but to their quality and the importance of the few cases in which they carried their disagreement beyond the conference table. Also, quite contrary to the popular notion, relatively few of all dissents recorded in the Supreme Court have later become law, although some of these are of great importance.[1]

Sometimes Supreme Court opinions contain materials which are not pertinent to the basic issues of the case. In other words, in the course of rendering an opinion, a justice may wander away from the major points of the case and make remarks that are not essential to the reasoning or decision. In legal terminology such remarks are known as obiter dicta, meaning that which was put in by the way or incidentally. Although obiter dicta do not establish principles of law, they may provide insights into a justice's personal views or indicate the development of particular judicial trends.

Supreme Court opinions are available in three separate editions.

(1). United States Reports (cited as U. S.) This is the official edition of Supreme Court cases and is published by the federal government. Usually the opinions of each term of the Court can be incorporated in two or three volumes of the Reports. Until 1875, the reports of Supreme Court decisions were cited by the name of the authorized reporter as follows:

1789-1800	Dallas (Dall.)	4 volumes
1801-1815	Cranch (Cr.)	9 volumes
1816-1827	Wheaton (Wheat.)	12 volumes

[1] Robert H. Jackson, *The Supreme Court in the American System of Government* (Cambridge: Harvard University Press, 1955), pp. 18-19.

1828-1842	Peters (Pet.)	16 volumes
1843-1860	Howard (How.)	24 volumes
1861-1862	Black (Bl.)	2 volumes
1863-1874	Wallace (Wall.)	23 volumes
1875-1882	Otto	17 volumes

The total number of volumes cited by the name of the reporter is ninety. After 1874, and beginning with Volume 91, the official reports are cited by number only.

(2). United States Supreme Court Reports, Lawyers' Edition (cited as L.ED.) This edition is privately published by the Lawyers' Cooperative Publishing Company. One volume ordinarily contains all of the decisions of one term of the Court. Both the Lawyers' Edition and the Supreme Court Reporter listed below contain more detailed headnotes than the official United States Reports. The headnotes, which appear at the beginning of the opinion, are designed to summarize the legal contents of the case. Those that appear in the two privately published editions are prepared by editorial staffs. Their purpose is to assist lawyers to obtain quickly comprehensive summaries of the case law in a particular subject matter. The Lawyers' Edition of the Supreme Court Reports also carries excerpts from the briefs of counsel and annotations of important cases.

(3). Supreme Court Reporter (cited as Sup. Ct.). This edition, which is similar to the Lawyers' Edition, is published by West Publishing Company. It is not a complete edition, however, since it contains only Supreme Court cases decided since 1882.

Citation of Cases. In citing cases, the volume number comes first, followed by the abbreviated title of the report in which the case appears and the page number, with the date in parentheses at the end. For example, the complete citation for the important recent case of *Baker* v. *Carr*, decided in 1962, is 369 U.S. 186; 7L.ed. 2d.633; 82 Sup. Ct. 691 (1962). This means that the full text of the Baker case may be found in Volume 369 of the United States Reports at page 186, or in Volume 7 of the Lawyers' Edition 2d at page 633 or in Volume 82 of the Supreme Court Reporter at page 691. The citation for *Marbury* v. *Madison* is 1 Cranch 137; 2 L.ed. 60, (1803). The case can therefore be found in Volume 1 of Cranch at page 137 or in Volume 2 of the Lawyers' Edition at page 60.

One need not wait until the bound volumes appear to read the full text of a Supreme Court case. Decisions of great public significance such as the Baker Case are often reproduced in full by some leading newspapers such as *The New York Times*. Also, the federal government publishes each decision in pamphlet or advance-sheet form as Preliminary Prints. These advance sheets appear about five to eight weeks after the decision is rendered. The two private publishers also issue advance sheets, which appear much earlier than those of the federal government. Complete opinions are available on the Tuesday following the Monday decision in the United States Law Week, published by the Bureau of National Affairs, and in the Supreme Court Bulletin, published by Commerce Clearing House.

The title of each case is taken from the names of the two parties to the controversy. The name that appears first is the party which is bringing the action, or the plaintiff. The defendant is the other party, against whom the action is taken. The v. between the two parties is simply an abbreviation for "versus" or against. Sometimes, as in the Merryman Case in Chapter 1, the case is entitled *Ex parte Merryman* when no other party is directly involved in the proceeding. Ex parte is a Latin term meaning simply "on the part of" or "from the side of." Hence, an ex parte legal proceeding is one which is undertaken without notice to any other party or parties. Also, as in the Yamashita case in Chapter 8, a case which does not involve two adversary parties of the usual kind may be entitled *In re Yamashita* meaning "in the matter of" Yamashita.

INDEX

Index

Date Due